MARKETING ME

MARKETING
ME
TAKE CHARGE
OF YOUR PERSONAL BRAND
AND MAKE YOUR MARK ON THE WORLD
NINA CHRISTIAN

 A catalogue record for this book is available from the National Library of Australia

First published in 2024 by Hambone Publishing
Melbourne, Australia

Editing by Mish Phillips, Lexi Wight, Laura McCall and Alex Hagan
Typesetting and design by David W. Edelstein

For information about this title, contact:
Nina Christian
support@ninachristian.com
www.ninachristian.com

ISBN 978-1-922357-58-8 (paperback)
ISBN 978-1-922357-59-5 (eBook)

This book is dedicated to my five beautiful children.

*You are precious gifts that brighten my world and inspire me
to always want to do my best, and be my best.*

*In different ways, you have all helped me discover more
about my own true identity, just by being who you are.*

*I know this world will be a better place for having each of
you in it, and I have so much admiration, love,
and gratitude for each of you.*

Contents

Preface

I zipped up my suitcase and drifted down to the meeting room. It was the final day of the retreat, and I was packed and ready to head back to the airport after the closing session.

The retreat was run by one of my business mentors – yet over the entire time, there hadn't been any conversation about my business or my work, much less my book, of which at the time, not a single word had yet been written.

As we concluded our time together, each of us attending randomly selected a card from a deck of inspirational messages.

"In times of trouble, remember this:
who you think you are cannot handle this
challenge, but who you really are can and will."
— Louise Hay

When I thought about what this message might mean for me, I assumed it had something to do with going home to a busy home life, my children, my work and all the inherent activity involved with that. Although, to be fair, at the time I felt I was doing pretty well, all things considered. So, it no longer felt like the "challenge" it once did. So that led me to wondering, what was this message REALLY about?

When I was asked about the quote in front of the group and how it applied to me, I defaulted to "I don't know," to create the space to think. In that moment, I truly had no idea. When I was probed to go a bit deeper, to take a guess, my gut started speaking to me.

It felt random, but "maybe my book" I queried?

Suddenly, as I uttered those words, my calm, centred, chill demeanour changed in a flash as tears filled my eyes and croakiness filled my throat. With such a powerful and spontaneous emotional response, it was clear to all present that of course this was about my book. I immediately thought perhaps the challenge was about how I was going to incorporate writing something worth reading in the midst of parenting, while running a growing, thriving business, and looking after myself: that's already a full plate.

As a hands-on mother to five children, professional speaker, marketing strategist and mentor to teams, entrepreneurs, and experts around the world, to say my weeks are fairly full is an understatement. But over the years I've learned the art and science of building spaciousness into my life – so as the questions probed deeper, I realised that wasn't what scared me.

I've been at this long enough, to know myself, to know that as an "actionator" I'd find a way to write this book. I realised the challenge being referred to was more about what was going to be **IN** this book. It was not just about making it useful by including technical and practical information that you can apply and benefit from – but by ***making it something that I hope will change your life.***

This isn't the book I was originally planning to write. However, the shift that occurred in that moment was the catalyst for this book being one you are holding in your hands right now.

This book was supposed to be a book about marketing; a book that validated my knowledge, experience, and expertise in this space. And it kind of is. So, if you bought this book to become better at marketing you won't be disappointed. But it's also about so much more.

It's about discovering your identity.

It's about the power that rests behind that process.

It's about the impact you will create as a result of it.

The more I go along, I realise **THIS** is the really important stuff.

I have been longing to write a book that will inspire people to embrace and value their uniqueness and significance in the world and use that to create impact around them, but always with the asterisk of "eventually" attached to that desire. The insecure part of me felt that the "technical expert" had to come first, but the more I thought about it the more I realised that's not what the world needs right now. We don't need more information and we certainly don't need more experts telling us what to do.

Because what we need is within us.

So often we listen to the myriad of voices around us instead of valuing our own. This leads to our own voice, our message, our essence and expression being buried deep beneath, unable to shine and be seen in all its glory. When, in this time, this is exactly what the world needs to hear and see. It's what humans crave – more than tools or technology. We all crave connection, and when we embrace our true identity, that is when we are able to connect with people. In an era where anyone can write anything and insights are flying around fast and furiously, **connection is everything.**

When you harness the uniqueness, significance and intention that sits behind who you are and what you're communicating, it does the heavy lifting in attracting the right people to your message.

I have been on a journey over the last few years discovering my identity – and I've witnessed the power that this has had in my marketing, on my business, and yes, even in my personal life.

So, I want to start there. This book is about creating room for you to allow your identity to shine – and infuse it into all you do, because that's what makes up YOUR personal brand. Yes, there will be big focus on your marketing – but it will not be limited to that – my hope is that it will have a powerful impact on your profession, career, your business, and, beyond that, your life.

If you're ready to embark on this journey with me and,

through building your personal brand, to shine your light and inspire those around you, then these words are for you too:

"In times of trouble, remember this:
Who you think you are cannot handle this challenge,
***but who you really are** can and will."*

You CAN do this. And the "you" that you are becoming as you go on this journey WILL do this.

I believe in you.

Introduction

The times we are in are extraordinary.

We are seeing the biggest shifts we have seen in our lifetime around the way we live and do business.

The rate of change will continue to accelerate. It's not going to "settle down" – ever. There isn't a playbook for the times we are in. It's being created – by US.

We all need to approach this with curiosity, and with an explorer's mindset.

To be creators.

To create the future.

It's a courageous task, calling us to step up and deliver something beyond what we have before. It requires us to do things differently, as we see what's possible.

Having a personal brand that is clear, compelling and creates impact is a key part of that – for all of us moving forward – whether we are a business owner, leader, or employee. Leading in organisations or industries where people are looking to us to "show the way".

A personal brand requires us to step up and *embrace* all of who we are, and *be* all of who we are.

It has never been more important to get clear and confident about how you are showing up in the world, especially when you have a message that matters. A message that is going to improve people's lives – their businesses, and their futures.

If you're reading these words, you're probably someone who senses a deep call. Someone who is fuelled by purpose and who has the motivation to step into that purpose, to live it out. Your personal brand is a powerful vehicle that will help you do that.

In a world full of polarising opinions, people clamouring for their minute or more of fame, your voice needs to be heard. This can be a challenge, to be heard above the noise, which sometimes feels at full volume. But **just because the world is loud, doesn't mean you should be quiet.**

Instead, it's more important than ever to be visible for all the right reasons.

To be a leader.

To be a voice of hope.

To be a beacon of inspiration.

These are the things many are so desperately looking for right now.

Despite all the disruptions, when we approach marketing with curiosity and an explorer's mindset it's way more playful and refreshing – and yields the most tangible results. And because "results" is a word bandied about so freely, I want to articulate what I mean by that.

*"**Results**"* in a personal brand building context typically include:

- A more engaged and captivated community and network who want to hear from you.
- Greater number of 'right fit' & influential people in your network/audience/list.
- Inbound enquiries – people know what you do and they come **_to_** you.
- You are respected as a leading authority in your field by peers and other leaders.
- You are positioned as the premium choice in your space so you can charge more for your services or command a higher salary.
- Higher conversion rates of prospects to customers with the same effort.
- High-profile people want to collaborate with you, invite you to speak, feature you, put you in front of their audiences.
- Your customers stay with you longer, spend more, and refer you to others.

While all these things have a commercial focus the end goal is that they ultimately enable you and your message to be more widely known so you can help more people and have greater impact in the world. Whether you're an industry leader, entrepreneur, or corporate professional, when you have a powerful personal brand that "paves the way" you can do all of this with less "effort" – which makes everything more profitable and sustainable.

My purpose in writing this book is clear to me. I want my kids, and their kids, and other people's kids, to grow up in a world full of inspiring voices of strength and substance, a world with a plethora of aspirational role models. And so, what I do in my business is part of my contribution to that, helping people with a mission that matters become visible as those aspirational role models – not just for their audiences and the world at large, but for their families and communities as well.

While the ability to have massive impact is there, as is the desire to make it happen, there is also the practical side – of actually doing it and getting that message in front of the right people. And the reality is that's where a lot of people get stuck.

They don't know how to go about becoming more widely known and get overwhelmed by the endless possibilities and conflicting advice that is out there, much of which just doesn't feel "natural".

It's time for us to approach marketing in a more human way, a way that *feels good to us,* and to our audience. Many people desire to do that – but not many know where to start.

The good news is that building a clear and compelling personal brand doesn't have to deplete you, instead it can energise you and give you a greater zest for life. Not only because that's what requires the least effort – and I'm all about ease - but because we all have a full life beyond our business that we want to have energy for. This is a fresh, liberating approach to marketing without the "shoulds" and "oughts". Let's not have those anymore. They don't serve us or come from a place of freedom, they have inherent judgement within them leading us to do things out of a sense of obligation, making things feel like a chore.

If your marketing isn't lighting you up, it's not lighting up people around you and that's what people are looking for now: they want to be lit up and they need people who will lead the way.

My intention with this book is to give you the spark to light you up. If you're already burning, that's great, my intention is to fan the flame, so your light shines brighter. This will help you give people something they can truly connect with.

Building a powerful personal brand isn't just about getting your message and products in front of more people, it's about connecting with your audience in a deeper more emotional way and to do that it's necessary to make people feel something with your marketing.

The concept of marketing in a way that "feels good" to you and to your audience sounds nice in theory, but in reality, living it out is where the transformation comes. If you choose to market yourself authentically, you're in for an exciting ride; sharing your true self with the world will grow you, expand you, and refine your character. However, it's not for the faint-hearted, embarking on this voyage will demand courage from you. Marketing yourself authentically will stretch you, but that stretch will propel you to amazing places in life and open possibilities beyond what you could imagine.

The journey to authentic personal branding won't just grow

your business and career, it will change your life. I know how powerful it can be and it's 100% worth it. It will lead you to feel good about how you're showing up in the world, knowing you're inspiring people as you do it, all while living out your purpose in this life.

The approach discussed in this book is not based around some flashy marketing hack or system because that's not where the power is. This work goes deeper because it's about embracing your true identity and getting clear on how to express that to the world. The hope is that instead of feeling the constant compulsion to "do" all the time, you have an impact just by "being" your authentic self. Embracing your unique identity and marketing yourself through personal branding is a surprisingly effective way of uncovering it.

When you embrace your true identity, and express that authentically and elegantly, you go from "making an impact" to "being impactful" wherever you go, and it feels so natural.

The former requires effort, but all the latter requires is YOU. Your identity is what powers your impact. More than your ambitions, hard work, tenacity, and expertise.

Your identity matters.
Your story matters.
You matter.

Through the tapestry of your life, the experiences you have and the stories you tell about them become the bridges that span generations.

Think about how the world would be different if you weren't here.

I love this quote. It's often used in corporate settings, but I love the extension to the personal brand.

"IF YOUR BRAND DISAPPEARED TOMORROW, WHAT WOULD THE WORLD BE MISSING?"[1]

This. Question. Is. Everything.

Magical, actually.

For anyone who thinks a brand is how you look, maybe even your expertise, radical-ness or brilliance...

Think again...

It's 100% about the world being improved by your brand and your conviction.

The quote above is a call to action to play the bigger game. It's not in service to the world to hold back the impact, inspiration, and empowerment you have to offer for fear of standing out. That's what I want for my brand, and that's what I want you to have the opportunity to create as well.

Because when the world is your oyster, embodying the answer to this question is the key to how you become that pearl.

So, if you're ready to **get clear, energised, and confident about how you are showing up in the world,** and marketing your business and yourself, I'm glad you're here and I'm honoured to help you do it through this book.

PART I

WHY BUILD A PERSONAL BRAND

CHAPTER 1
The New Era of Marketing

The distant sound of a motorbike revving up signalled the impending arrival of the postman. As a young girl playing in the front yard for hours on end during school holidays, one of the highlights of my day was fantasising about what might be in the bright yellow bag on that bike. Something for me, perhaps? For a few short minutes, as the sound of the engine drew closer, the anticipation would grow, until I would run down the big hill to collect the mail.

I was the kind of kid that had "pen pals" (who remembers those?) and so it was fairly usual for me to receive a colourful envelope complete with glitter and scratch 'n' sniff stickers all over it. One of those was usually enough to make my day.

The best surprises were the letters from faraway family members, complete with the familiar handwriting of a loved one, news from their life, and that warmth, love and connection that was felt as the letter was read. My favourite, however, were the letters from grandma, with the decorative cursive font on the envelope and the occasional memento slipped into the envelope. But those days were few and far between. I'll always remember that feeling of disappointment running down the hill only to find bills.

To this day, these memories still remind me of how we relate to brands – whether they are business brands or people brands. There are plenty of brands and messages we block out, even if they are legitimate. BUT there are also others we can't wait to hear from. It's not always about the content in those messages, it's most often about how they make us feel.

The tone, feeling, value, and consistency in the way they show up, and the commitment to share something fresh, insightful, and motivating – caring, even, is what stays with us. Just like my letters from grandma, these are the brand messages I most look forward to.

Too often, marketing is transactional, impersonal, and forgettable. In a sea of electricity bills, be a letter from Grandma.

Marketing is in Flux

The traditional marketing playbook is no longer working.

Before we discuss how to adapt and evolve our marketing, it's essential to understand WHY so much has changed. This will help us understand the importance of a different approach behind building an authentic personal brand that resonates and inspires people to action.

Every single person is trying to process a raft of challenges that impact at both a global and deeply personal level.

There are three distinct areas of "more".

Traditional methods of marketing are no longer cutting it. If you feel like you're slogging through mud, talking to an audience of crickets, or feeling confused and flustered you're not alone. With people tuning out, feeling fatigued, and becoming more selective about how they spend their time and money, and where they put their attention, the appetite and tolerance for marketing messages has plummeted.

But here's the good news: people are still open to connecting. They want to feel seen, heard, and supported, and they're looking for brands that can deliver that emotional connection. To do that, we need to shift our approach. Our audiences are not just numbers to be marketed to, and each interaction is not just a "lead to be converted". The key to success is establishing meaningful connections with your audience, as people.

So, how do you establish meaningful connections? It's not just about having "useful" information to share, fancy photoshoots, or whiz-bang copywriting skills. The secret is to connect with your authentic identity in a deep way, so that everything you do with your marketing is congruent and strategic. When you successfully do this people don't just notice you, they form a deep bond with and are drawn to you.

This might sound odd if you've only consumed mainstream internet marketing gurus over the last few years. But as a marketer of almost three decades, I can tell you that this is where we are right now.

The marketing that makes YOU feel good is also the marketing that will resonate with your audience.

MORE CHANGE than ever before.

The world has changed. Society has changed. People have changed.

In the last few years we've had the greatest health, economic, and humanitarian crises that hopefully any of us will see in our lifetime. The economics textbook has been thrown out because conventional knowledge has met unprecedented circumstances. Identity politics has polarised opinions and even families. Rates of depression, anxiety, burnout, and fatigue are skyrocketing. There is deep concern and uncertainty about how AI will shape our professions and lives.

Each of these is another track that's playing in our minds.

Our mental bandwidth has shifted. As we juggle more, feel more, and change more, it's clear we're in the midst of a revolution that's changing the way we think, feel and make decisions. This means we need to do things differently for our audiences as well. People's habits, mindsets, and purchasing behaviours have changed drastically in the last few years alone. However much we might want it to stabilise, in the words of Justin Trudeau, Prime Minister of Canada: "The pace of change has never been this fast, yet it will never be this slow again."

This pace of change is critical to factor in when marketing our products or services, particularly in a digital environment. The need to "think different," as Steve Jobs, the founder of Apple, often said, and being ultra-strategic has never been more important than it is today. It's important to note that this isn't just a knee-jerk response to specific shifts such as the post-lockdown world, or the proliferation of artificial intelligence. It's a way of thinking that's curious, open and adaptable, so that we are able to evolve as the world around us is evolving.

I discovered the power of this co-evolutionary mindset at the height of my marketing agency's success in 2018. Braveda, the marketing agency which I founded in 2000, was achieving industry recognition, being awarded *Marketing Agency of the Year* at the *Australian Marketing Excellence Awards*. We had a large focus on content and strategy as well as top-notch execution and were devoted to developing top talent in our industry. But it was then that I also realised that much of traditional marketing was missing the mark. This led me on a journey of exploration that opened a whole new trajectory.

In 2019, I made the decision to transition away from running a traditional style marketing agency and began to reduce staff and clients. And in 2020, I hung up my marketing agency boots after 20 years of being in service to brands around the globe, helping them create an impact. It didn't make complete sense to anyone, apart from myself.

Many felt that the recent accolades I had received in the years prior would be a springboard to creating a bigger agency. I had just won *Marketing Agency of the Year* and the same year I'd won *Certified Practicing Marketer (CPM) of the Year (Vic)*. And it wasn't that there isn't a place for marketing agencies anymore. On the contrary, I train and mentor many of them today! But for me, the decision was driven by something different.

What motivated me was realising that despite my more than twenty years of running an agency, as well as my professional development, marketing experience, teaching and implementing, working on my own marketing, content, and systems – something was lacking. And I had a deep desire to find and explore it.

The missing piece was the role of *identity* – and not just organisational identity, but personal identity. People were separating business and personal, but it became clear that the two were enmeshed. Business was deeply personal.

So, I wound down a business that was at the peak of its game to pursue a deep dive into exploring the art and science of building an impactful personal brand for commercial purposes. I now teach this to businesses, marketers, and leaders around the world.

MORE NOISE than ever before

Most people in the world are exposed to thousands of marketing messages each day[2], even though we only register a few and filter the majority out. This includes various types of advertising such as online (in a multitude of different types, everything from pop ups to banners, and social media ads), out of home (billboards, transport and signage), television commercials, product placement, email marketing, content, radio, print materials, and product packaging, among others. With the increasing use of digital media and the proliferation of mobile devices, the number of marketing messages is continually increasing.

Over and above marketing messages, the number of people in our sphere (definitely online, maybe offline too) has likely increased. We are expected to be present in more areas of life and keep up with an ever-changing world, meaning our brains are constantly making decisions, whether we realize it or not. Which information do I let in? What do I screen out? Who can I trust? What do I need to know? What about those I'm responsible for? How do I preserve my sanity through it all?

MORE INFORMATION than ever before

Imagine you're standing in the middle of Times Square as an unending rush of bright, flashy billboards vie for your attention. Each one louder and more insistent than the last. The intensity of the lights, sounds, and movement overwhelms your senses with an onslaught of information from every direction. The reality is you don't need to go all the way to New York to experience that, you just need to have a phone and a laptop. There's a ceaseless onslaught of information bombarding us from every corner of our digital lives, 24/7. We're all living in Times Square.

And this "content overload" is only going to get more intense in the years to come, as it becomes technologically possible for more brands to reach bigger audiences, and as more and more people (and machines!) clamour for our attention. As a result, our ability to retain volumes of information is diminishing as so much of it is coming our way each day. This is important to keep in mind as we are building a presence that is visible to more people. Simply being aware that your message is likely mixed in with thousands of other messages coming at them simultaneously is essential.

Regardless of where your audience is located, there isn't a place on earth that hasn't been turned upside down in the last few years. People in general are cynical about many of the old ways of becoming visible, especially when it comes to content and messaging, and they remember less of what they see and hear. Therefore, our approach needs to change, as messaging precision and emotional connection become vital ingredients in being seen, heard, and remembered.

So, what does this mean when it comes to marketing?

"Adding value" is no longer the gold standard, especially when it comes to content creation.

(If you skimmed over that previous line, I'll repeat it, it's important!)

"ADDING VALUE" IS NO LONGER THE GOLD STANDARD

We are now in an era where there is "value" everywhere we look – Google, YouTube, infographics in your social feed – heck, even the local library! Free valuable information on every topic imaginable is widely available and no longer hard to find, there is more than you could ever consume in a lifetime. What is lacking is the ability to interpret that information and break down which of the gazillion ideas is worth applying, and what is genuinely helpful to an individual's unique situation at a particular point of time.

On top of that, making this accessible and actionable for the average person with a business, or a job, kids or pets, who values self-care, relationships, and their sanity, is an even bigger challenge. The volume of information we desire to be aware of increases, but our mental bandwidth to process it diminishes due to the myriad of things competing for our attention. When people are tuning out because of too much on their mind, we need to stop playing the volume game.

Relieving anxiety with the content we create, not creating more of it, should be the goal. So that instead of that feeling of being a constant stream of paparazzi flashes in the eyes of our audience, who are struggling to take it all in, our content is more akin to the trusted lamp of an air traffic controller in the night, clearly visible and showing the way to the runway and helping them take off and get to where they want to go faster, and safely.

In a world that's obsessed with value and volume, audiences just want to be shown the way.

The Authenticity Filter is ON

Humans are very smart, yet we are created with an instinctual nature, which extends beyond the rational.

The rational mind has served us very well for a long time. But right now, the sheer volume that our already-overloaded brains are trying to process on a day-to-day basis can be overwhelming. Not to mention the newest wave of considerations – is this originating from a human or an intelligent machine? Is this real, true – or is it made to look like this to get us to pay attention? And the vastness of information coming at us, and the volume of micro-decisions that we are required to make is not slowing down. So – what's a human to do?

Something we've been doing for eons, when our rational mind doesn't have access to all the information, we need to make a logical decision. We rely on our *intuition.* The part of us that "just knows" if something is legit or not. It's aways been there and some people have operated in it more fully than others. Of the many changes that humanity went through during the most recent pandemic it was an elevation in perceptiveness – at a much wider-scale that saw more people lean into their intuition, spirituality, and emotions as they made decisions.

This is the reality of marketing that all brands need to contend with. And it's only going to be more prevalent in the future as the current flow of information becomes untenable and people opt-out even further with heightened sensors around what they're prepared to "let in" to their world.

Ditching FOMO & Scarcity

After a rough few years globally that pushed mental health, resilience, and hyper-awareness to new levels, people are craving security, comfort, and hope and so are now generally resisting fear-based, scarcity and pressure-led messaging that was commonplace in the decades prior. Not all brands operated this way, but many did as a means to create demand for their product or service.

These days, with the proliferation of new brands entering the marketplace, using old-school tactics to clamour for attention, the average person has become so jaded and as a result, averse to pesky people with flaky marketing, obtrusive offers, problematic products, and fear mongering. So many brands (especially in the online space) who led with this type of marketing are now being pushed away and ignored, and rightly so. Because, while the struggle may be real, people don't need to be reminded of it over and over again.

Our inboxes, news feeds, mainstream media, social feeds, and web browsing have had way too much:

- Scarcity,
- FOMO,
- Worst-case scenarios,
- Grim statistics,
- Fake/outdated testimonials,
- Bot generated "insights" masked as personal content,
- ...the list goes on.

Getting attention, attracting the right audience, building trust, and turning fans into customers has become more of a challenge than ever before for many brands – both personal and business brands.

This is especially the case because the old playbook isn't working like it used to and trying to deploy outdated tactics and get ROI on them often leaves anyone building a personal brand feeling frustrated and depleted – this can be a major energy suck.

This is doubly unfortunate as it is occurring right at the time when it's critical to conserve and use our energy wisely. Because when we are the brand, we need it for our personal wellbeing more than ever!

Our collective brain is craving relief, comfort, and gentleness and so, for those who are leading with a different approach, there is huge opportunity.

When it comes to building a personal brand, it's important to avoid the following:

1. Doing the same as you did in the past.

The tactics may still be effective, but they may have passed their "best before" date in their old-school format, so if you're doing them the same way you did a year ago, with similar content and messaging, and it isn't working, don't be surprised.

2. Hiring someone who knows little about your business to "produce content" in the effort to be seen.

This is a sure-fire recipe to waste time and money and leave you frustrated. Good content just isn't enough when you're a personal brand – these days it needs to be content that emanates from YOU, to stand out and attract people to engage with it.

3. Doing an assortment of random things, hoping people will just find their way into your world.

It's tempting to think that activity alone will generate results but it can actually be damaging to your brand, not to mention your personal energy. While you might get lucky, the majority of people don't, and chances are you'll end up feeling jaded after putting in effort for that things aren't working and yielding commercial results.

CHAPTER 2

The Great Marketing Reset

Marketing is a New Ballgame

The first big wave of change I lived through as a professional marketer was the introduction of the internet to the mainstream way of doing business in the 1990's. I still remember the first time I saw a "website". I was in my boss's office at my first job, a tourism retailer in Sydney in 1995. The marketing team crowded around the Marketing Manager's computer, ogling, ooh-ing and ahh-ing at this magical page from a futuristic new outfit *Citysearch,* feeling like we had been zapped into a sci-fi movie, and instinctively feeling that life as we know it is about to change forever.

Blown away, I decided to show my family, and so when I next visited my parents, we grabbed a cup of tea and headed to in the spare room and watched in fascination as that same *Citysearch* page made its way, line by line onto the screen via a

28.8k modem connection. I remember us all freaking out how that within about 4 minutes the colourful page was magically displayed on a monitor at a suburban house via a cable.

The first web browser was released in 1993. The world wide web (Web 1.0) ushered in a new era of how we live and do business. It was primarily about dissemination of information and the introduction of blogs, online media, and websites where publishers could disperse information to the public. Then in the mid-2000's the next great change unfolded, the era of social media, and user-generated content and sharing and exchange of information (Web 2.0). No longer was the internet the domain of publishers, and access to information and opportunity quickly democratised. Now, Web 3.0 is decentralising the ownership of information and is shifting the balance of power and the way it is stored, shared, and governed.

If Web 1.0 was about dispersal of information into the world and Web 2.0 was about the world co-creating information, Web 3.0 is about creating entire new worlds in the digital environment using platforms such as blockchain technology, impacting finance, community, entertainment, social interaction, and businesses. Web 3.0 is changing things in a massive way, as assets digitise, AI adoption skyrockets, realities merge, communities disperse across new platforms, and methods of transacting evolve.

Despite the profound influence of technology, the biggest change of all is not about new tech tools, platforms, and the proliferation of artificial intelligence. **It's not the evolution**

of technology, but the evolution of humanity that will most impact our future.

This change is significant because it's more about people and the changes that our collective psyche has gone through over the recent years. Audiences have changed because people have changed. The rules are changing too, constantly.

So how do we adapt when the only constant is change[3], and what does this mean for growing our brands, especially personal brands, when the brand is "us"?

There is No Playbook

Nobody has it completely figured out. If anyone tells you there's a guaranteed way to do anything, and that they "know the way," you will see right through them. The reality is that there are no true experts who know everything there is to know about any domain right now – because each and every domain is rapidly expanding – and changing – marketing included.

The thing about being an "expert" is there's a temptation to talk a big game and have it all figured out. But with the pace of change we're experiencing, it's about the principles rather than the specific practices – and being able to adapt them skilfully and intuitively for a constantly changing landscape. As author and industry colleague Mark Schaefer aptly says: *"Any hope of expertise has been overrun by the malignant complexity of our world."*[4]

That said, there is no shortage of "experts" out there offering advice and solutions right now. I guess you could say I'm one of them – the irony of the fact that I'm writing a book to guide you on something we're all figuring out right now is not lost on me!

The most effective approach is ***gently feeling forward*** – consciously surrendering to the fact that things ARE constantly changing – and remaining curious, flexible and gently adapting to how things evolve. Testing, being open, adapting, and experimenting. Sharing the discoveries and the lessons with our peers, community and industry.

If you're feeling like you wish you could just follow "the plan" there isn't one. Sorry. "The playbook" doesn't exist. But that's also exciting, because it means we get to create our own path forward – and as a personal brand your path is going to be unique to you!

The Rise of the Feeling

There is currently a massive shift back to a form of marketing that has a deep personal connection. And by this, I mean the creation of content that has the ability to make people ***feel something.*** You're likely familiar with the oft-quoted words: *"People will forget what you said, people will forget what you did, but people will never forget how you made them feel."*[5] This is so true in our marketing and the way we communicate with those in our business sphere.

Right now, our collective brain is craving relief, comfort, and gentleness. We don't want to be spoken "at" – we want to be seen, and heard, and have our feelings and mental state validated.

While there are a lot of ways to do this, and they could involve conducting research, consulting with psychologists, analysts and focus groups, many personal brands don't have the resources or capacity to do a deep dive into the psychological state, needs and drivers of their audience.

I like to break it down and make things super simple to understand and easy to apply. And when it comes to how our marketing makes people feel – there's a very simple filter to put over it that can give us a really good gauge: ***Will someone feel better after reading/watching/listening to this?***

With attention fleeting and scarce, people are naturally more attracted to brands that make them feel better about themselves. It wasn't always like this, and it may change again at some stage in the future, but right now people are craving hope, inspiration, and encouragement.

I realise this may not seem like a deep message, but I can assure you, it's powerful. It's one I'll hang my hat on, because I'm proof it works. I run this filter over everything I publish and while I know I'm not the most eloquent, polished, or prolific communicator, people constantly tell me (and other people) about how what I write makes them feel something, why it moves them, and why they feel safe and secure reading and applying it. Often that leads to other business opportunities, but that's not the primary intention. I do it this way because I believe this is what people need from brands and leaders right now. And above all, because this approach feels good to me too. And when I feel good about how I'm showing up and what I'm sharing as a personal brand, I know my audience feels that too.

The new reality is these things are equally important in modern marketing:

- **How you make your audience feel** as they engage with your marketing and content.
- **How YOU feel** about yourself as you create and provide content, and see your brand reflected in the marketplace.

Because that speaks volumes. And people pick it up.

Be the person (and brand) they look forward to hearing from; like the letter from grandma.

Empathy over Expertise

A lack of consideration of the human psyche is one of the big failings of modern marketing. Many marketing strategies have a go-for-the-jugular approach where they try to seal the deal from the first touchpoint, while others have some cookie-cutter "affinity-building" approach that is as shallow as the dish it was baked in. This has led to viewer fatigue and a natural numbness to these aggressive marketing techniques. And a by-product of that is the sheer volume of content they are exposed to means they are often less receptive to "good" marketing too.

The single biggest shift in personal brand marketing this

decade is the fact that sharing Information and your knowledge (even if it's brilliant) isn't enough anymore. Not if you want to build a genuine relationship with your audience. But if you actually *care* enough about how your customers might be feeling to actually meet them where they're at, you have a better than average chance of getting through to them.

Marketing should not just be about throwing out solutions either; a content-fatigued audience is over that. The biggest mistake I see people make in their effort to demonstrate "value" is producing truckloads of "how to" content to showcase their expertise in an area. Basically, this "how to" content is information people can google. It can be useful, but not the most impactful form of content and often leads to people producing a wide variety of "information," diluting their master message. It's not overly unique, nor does it lead people to feel deeply connected to you, or to buy from you.

"The best marketing strategy ever. Care."
— Gary Vaynerchuck

You can share the best thought leadership and insights, but if YOU don't care about your audience and building connection, they won't care about your great information. They'll nod their head, just like they do with all the other hundreds of insightful and knowledge-filled posts they see each day, lump you in the same category, and move on. If you don't layer your thought leadership and "expert advice" with genuine empathy your marketing is probably falling on deaf ears.

It's not just about "saying" the right things either, it's about actually caring. The days of people being able to "front" on social media are over. The average consumer is way savvier than they used to be, their BS detectors are so finely attuned.

With so much knowledge out there flooding the market-place, who's to say yours is better? That's not what's going to form the bond between your brand and your customer – but standing for something, and truly caring about them, is.

Setting the right intention before and as you create a piece of content or any marketing initiative is created is supremely powerful, and not just from a strategy perspective but from a deep sense of understanding. As Vietnamese Monk Thích Nhất Hạnh famously said, *"Understanding is love's other name."* This is true even in marketing right now.

People are craving hope, optimism, and, quite simply, the need to "feel good" and "feel seen" in the face of a million things trying to get them down. If your brand can play that role – you will be one that's remembered.

It you want to go beyond just communicating, and truly connect, be the brand that relieves rather than creates anxiety.

Walk a mile in their shoes, or rather, sit for an hour in their inbox or news feed. What's on their mind? What's the big goal they're currently trying to nail? Why? Where are they looking for answers? Why is what they're doing not working? And how does what you are sharing help them alleviate that?

Think of it from your own experience as a consumer, what kind of marketing makes you feel good? It's the stuff that brightens your day, puts a spring in your step, or a shot of confidence that you've got this.

How do you do this in a way that's commercially smart? By finding the aspects of the messaging that are both strategic for your business AND deliver a huge dose of encouragement to your audience. This way, they will be way more receptive to what you have to say. And they might not be ready to buy from you right now, but you'll be the memorable choice when the right time comes.

Plus, you'll be making the world just that little bit brighter for someone in the process. And that definitely makes you feel good and motivates you to show up and create content more often.

I like to ask this question: Can you make your marketing messages feel like a warm, reassuring hug? Sounds contradictory, but this is the marketing of the future.

Run it through this very simple lens: Will someone feel better after reading/ watching/ listening to this? If not, you might want to re-think it right now.

Does your content have "soul"?

This wasn't a question we thought much about a few years ago – we just needed to ensure our content was high quality, relevant, and valuable. Moving forward, the ability to truly connect, and move people with our content is where it's at.

Think about your marketing content like music. When we

think about "soul music" – we think about music that makes us feel. When you listen to the undisputed Queen of Soul, Aretha Franklin and her classics, you feel the energy behind it. It's palpable. Whether it's *R.E.S.P.E.C.T* or *(You Make Me Feel Like) A Natural Woman*, she's got it.

It's all about the feels.

And so is connecting with your audience (aka marketing) right now. Because if it isn't – people are tuning out, glossing over, or switching off, thinking: oh that's nice, but I'm too busy to read/listen/watch/take action.

I was working with a global figure in the wellbeing space, with thousands of customers, tens of thousands in her audience.

*"I'm sick of putting out soul-less sh*t"* she lamented.

"When I see your content" she continued, *"it makes me stop".*

"And I don't usually "read" content, but I read yours. I have to!"

"And I want my audience to have this type of 'thump in the chest content' too." she said.

This is someone who published weekly blogs, had social media content scheduled half a year in advance, had worked with tons of high-end copywriters, had a large email database, and a laundry list of high-profile worldwide media appearances. On the surface, many would say she was nailing it. Yet, despite all of this, she felt like there was a disconnect between her, her content, and how she was showing up in the marketplace, but she couldn't put her finger on it. She went on to say *"I don't want to appeal to everyone, but I want the right people to be so deeply connected to who I am and what I do."*

This is the feeling I see a lot in high-achievers who

frustratingly sense that what they are putting out doesn't match the depth and power that they know sits behind them as a person and as a brand. If you feel like that too, you're not alone.

It's not to say your content is inherently bad. Two years ago, it might have made the grade, maybe even have gotten an A. But right now, if you want to get people's attention, you need to run it through the lens of "Is it making people feel something?" Because if it isn't – people are tuning out, glossing over, or switching off.

Content with emotion is the "superhighway of connection" right now. There's nothing that comes close. This is how we connect with people now.

My client did the work and infused her essence and true identity into her content, and the business benefits she experienced within weeks were phenomenal: ad costs halved, 100x increase in the response rate to emails being sent out, lowest CPL (cost per lead) cost ever, highest conversion rate. There was nothing different about her business model, sales process, or promotional plan. The only thing that changed was how she was showing up as a brand, via her content, and injecting the essence of her soul, to connect with them. I was so pleased to lead her through this process and help her take a leaf out of Aretha's book: R.E.S.P.E.C.T. your audience, find out what it means to them, infuse your 'soul' and sock it to 'em.

Sure, you can give them your best – most inspiring, action-inducing, mindset-shifting, hope-fuelling insights but above all, do it in a way that makes them FEEL something.

CHAPTER 3
Big Shifts in Branding

Your brand is the emotional connection you create with your audience through everything you do.

Rewind a decade or two and it was all about the logo. People felt like they needed a logo to be reputable, credible, and taken seriously. I know the discomfort of this transition and the downright discomfort of putting yourself out there as a "personality".

Twenty years ago, when I co-founded a startup during the dot com boom, there was a flurry of media interest and I was routinely speaking to journalists for interviews. I often conceded to an interview but requested they didn't publish a photo or name; I wanted my privacy. That was until a journalist for a national magazine straight up rebuked me saying I couldn't have it both ways, I couldn't represent a brand but remain nameless. I accepted that and cajoled myself with the fact at least no photos would be published. So, in the eight years from when the brand was born, to when it was sold, even with all the international press, TV, radio, magazine and online coverage, there wasn't a single photo associating me or my co-founder with it.

For years I also hid behind a marketing agency company logo – and that was fine back then – until it wasn't. When people suddenly shifted and developed a keen interest in who is behind the brand, I was forced to change my ways. I'll admit, it was hard. All of a sudden, the voluminous accolades about how long you've been in business, the credentials, all the things you've done and clients you've served were replaced in large part by:

- What do you stand for?
- Do I like you?
- Can I trust you?
- Do you care about me?

The Connected Brand

At its core, the strength of your most powerful, connected brand is the holistic combination of:

You can have the most polished, professional, and beautiful looking brand but that doesn't mean your content will connect.

A decade ago, we had way less resources – these days with the latest apps, not to mention AI, everyone has access to tools that can make their designs look professional with very little effort.

A flow on effect from this is that now the expectation is higher as well, the general population is more aware of trends around colours, visuals, brand styles, and cohesion. The bar is higher and it's not the polished visuals that garner your brand respect or connection anymore.

It's the combination of these four elements working together. Let's look at each of them briefly:

VISUALS – What Is "Seen"

Visual cohesiveness is important. It's a way to increase brand recognition and be memorable. If you don't have a distinct look and feel to your brand you miss out on opportunities to be noticed and give people a consistent visual experience.

Communicating your brand essence through strategic use of visual elements – among which are colours, graphical elements, fonts, images, filters, and formatting is effective. Usually these will be outlined in a Brand Book or Brand Style Guide which will help you or anyone working on your brand remain consistent in how you are presenting online. Think of this as guard rails to keep you on track.

Corporations have these out of necessity because so many people work on the brand – I've worked with brands that have style guides in the hundreds of pages because of the need to be so precise!

For a personal brand something very basic will suffice. The key is ensuring it's a congruent expression of who you are, not just a combination of randomly selected colours, fonts and assets that have no bearing on who you are and how you express yourself.

For personal brands, the parameters of brand expression

are generally a lot looser. The brand identity and style guide is still an anchor but with less rigidity, as people want to see wider and multi-faceted expressions of a brand, especially personal brands, and this is great news because while you want to maintain general consistency it means you're not locked into something either.

Your brand is like you – unique, dynamic and ever-evolving!

VOICE – What Is "Heard"

Your Voice has to do with the personality, tonality, and character and even the signal of your brand.

Just like each human has a unique pattern that contributes to the distinctiveness of a person's voice, each personal brand has a distinct "brand voice" – not just to the "ear", but beyond that, vibrationally.

The vibrational pattern of the vocal cords depends on several factors, including the physical characteristics of the vocal cords themselves, as well as the overall anatomy and physiology of a person. These all contribute to the unique sound and quality of each voice, including its pitch, timbre, and resonance – and which is what makes each voice distinct and individually recognisable by software.

In Australia when we call the tax office one of the standard procedures we go through is saying the words "In Australia, my voice identifies me" – which is then verified to confirm our identity. A microphone turns vibrations of the human voice into an electrical signal, which is subsequently converted using software into a digital signal.

Just as every human voice is unique, based on their unique attributes, physiology, and frequency, so it is with your brand voice.

This is where you get to shine, most effortlessly. Talking the way you talk, using the language that's uniquely you, and embracing the quirks and personality traits that you embody in your everyday life as well.

And communicating in this authentic way whether you're talking in a video, presenting a speech, writing a book or blog, showing up on social or email. Every single expression of your message is carried by the voice and is a powerful way for people to feel like they know the "real you" – vital when you're a personal brand.

When you're a corporation it's necessary to have a strict code around what is and isn't ok to communicate as the "voice" of the brand. It's harder to capture, define, and adhere to as it's made up of so many diverse individuals.

When you're a personal brand it's much easier – it's just you being you!

VALUES – What Is "Felt"

This is where what's "behind the brand" is allowed to permeate in every expression. It's beyond what's seen and heard and goes to the heart and is what will determine if your message makes it through the "authenticity filter" your audience have switched on by default.

If there isn't alignment in what's motivating the action and intention, people pick that up and feel like there's something "off" even if they can't put their finger on it. So, congruency between the two is paramount.

It's where intentionality meets expression – where what truly sits behind the brand is made bare and picked up within the energetic field of the audience. It transcends intellect and is instinctive. It is a means of transmitting "intention" – although this happens mostly at an unconscious level – both by transmitter (brand) and receiver (audience).

This is a rapidly evolving area and one that has experienced a massive shift of late, so we'll devote a lot more to this area as we go along in the book.

VALUE – What Is "Done"

The fourth element of connected brands is that they focus on value. They know and enhance the tangible value that they bring into the world. How does what you do make people's lives better? This is where people consider and analyse the impact that your brand is making.

Does it deliver on the promise it makes? Your brand stands for something – does the service, experience and interaction stack up?

This is also where a lot of your marketing "lives" as you share things that matter, not just in marketing content and thought leadership, but in simple exchanges like emails, phone calls, sales transactions, customer experience's post-sale. All of it goes into how people are impacted when they interact with you as a brand.

Your
VISUALS
– Logo
– Colors
– Style
– Typography
– Imagery
What is "SEEN"
Your
VALUE
– Improving lives/business
– Customer Experiences
– Content & Community
– Thought Leadership
– Communications
– Delivering on the Brand Promise
What is "DONE"
Your
Powerful
Connected
BRAND
Your
VOICE
– Personality
– Tone
– Language
– Character
What is "HEARD"
Your
VALUES
– What's your "why"
– What you stand for
– What you live by
– Congruency
What is "FELT"

Things your brand is NOT ✖

Your:
- ✖ Logo
- ✖ Colours
- ✖ Graphics
- ✖ Fonts
- ✖ Tagline
- ✖ Fancy Packaging
- ✖ Signature "look"
- ✖ Filters and special effects
- ✖ Hip Urban Slang
- ✖ Promotional Merch

Yes, all of these contribute to what your brand communicates overall, but they're just a tiny part of it: the shop front. There is so much more for your audience to take in. A strong brand connects powerfully, it bonds you deeply with your customers, without you having to be pushy, quaint, quirky, or cute.

You don't have to be a marketer to build a brand

Many people I talk to believe that only people with lots of marketing experience can build a captivating personal brand. This is simply not true. **Finding what makes you unique and how to express that in the world is something *best done by you.***

It's like saying you need to be an accountant to do your household budget and manage your money. Of course, there are specialist things that an accountant would do, just like there are some things that a professional marketer would do. But the reality is, anyone can build a compelling personal brand when they have the right tools and processes.

You've got the hard part down pat: being extraordinary at what you do, knowing what you're called to do, and having a passion to lean into it and make it real. The rest is just details.

The Human Advantage

Humans as brands

People don't really care about your logo anymore. The days of having a nameless, faceless logo-driven brand are long-gone, and have morphed into us wanting to see the human face of whoever is at the helm and on the frontline.

If you're showing up consistently as a one-dimensional entity, you're missing out on so many connection points. Humans behave differently in different contexts; this is what we want from brands too.

People aren't interested in brands being formal, professional, and guarded. They're watching how they respond to mistakes, how caring they are, how they treat people, and how willing they are to be vulnerable and pull back the curtain for the purpose of inspiring them. Done in a smart, subtle, and strategic way, of course. For small businesses it means the founder needs to be more visible and vocal. For personal brands and solopreneurs, it means that they needed to be more confident in being their "true selves" and relinquishing the need for others to speak on their behalf or "outsource their voice".

They want to see *your* face and *your* personality and feel *your* brand energy.

People desire to experience the diverse and multifaceted personality of your brand, because if it's always the same one-dimensional communication eventually they'll glaze over and tune out.

They desire the same attributes in brands that they do in humans, namely:

- **Integrity**
- **Vulnerability**
- **Transparency**

People are craving for big brands to be more human, multi-dimensional too. They want to see them owning and growing through their inevitable mistakes. For larger corporations this transition has been the trickiest – as they deal with the challenge of brand ambassadors, and determining which staff members and spokespeople will resonate most with the public. They have to consider what happens when people move on, and be mindful that if they want to show "behind the scenes" as a way to connect with people, it needs to be real, not staged and filtered.

This is where the personal brand has the advantage: as we have the courage to show up and present however we like. To change and evolve, and bring people along on the journey of who we are becoming. It's not like we need to live our lives under a microscope; there are always parts that can, will and should remain private. I'm also most definitely not advocating for treating your marketing like therapy, sharing your unresolved traumas publicly and using it to garner sympathy. Even in the guise of "relatability". That will backfire on you personally, as well as on your brand. But it is important to be thoughtful about which elements of you (or your organisation) you feel comfortable injecting into your public brand persona. The bottom line is that there needs to be a willingness to share more than just the polished and professional front. And the parts that you do share need to be authentic and real.

For example, how I present in a board meeting will be very different to when I'm out with friends, and different again to when I'm hanging out at home with my kids. They are all "me" through and through – and I feel fully "myself" in each context. Using a personal example like this, it's easy to understand how a "person" can be more multi-faceted. And it's this that people are craving in brands as well. Not a one dimensional, "always the same" way of presenting, but one that embraces difference and uniqueness and reflects different aspects of the culture in a congruent way.

Where this takes us is into the unknown. But what is sure is that as machines proliferate reams of information and insights, the need to harness our brand energy and connect as humans will get stronger. Sharing our stories, our growth, and our personalities, and keeping connection as the main thing is essential, because that's what humans crave. Finding new ways to establish and deepen these connections is the big opportunity moving forward.

Brand Energy – The New Frontier

A powerful concept for the emerging era of building a brand is ***Brand Energy.***

It's where the metaphysical meets the mechanics of marketing. It's no longer just about having people know, like, and trust you, we need to delve deeper into quantum physics to embrace the powerful forces at play driving the "brand to audience" connection.

Unlike previous connection methods that could be curated via clever narrative, this one is exciting because it can't be faked. What sits behind the brand is coming up to the surface. This is amazing for a lot of good people out there but a bit scary for others. There is no more masking, no more faking, no more copying. Because the stakes are too high. It doesn't matter how clever or accomplished you are, people will pick up on your energy and it will attract or repel them on an intuitive level. They won't know why and probably nor will you – initially.

I'm not saying don't craft an awesome visual identity and pay attention to your words; this is not an either/or, it needs to be both/and. As a professional brand-builder, the importance of being strategic is hard-wired into my professional DNA, but it's not the full story. There's more. And this has accelerated recently based on how people have collectively evolved in the years following the pandemic.

The way we engage with audiences is changing so fast, not gently, not subtly – it's shifting dramatically. In many cases, it is completely upending how we do things.

It's not the basic principles of marketing that have changed. On the contrary, the timeless marketing principles around the need to be strategic, creative, and analytical remain. However, your message needs to be expressed in a different way to cut through, to meet audiences where they are at. Audiences are in a different place emotionally now than they were two years ago, regardless of when you're reading this! The way we connect with people and get our message out must adapt to that.

How brand energy works in a nutshell: like with anything you choose to embrace and become more familiar with; awareness is a great place to start. Being mindful that whatever you create or curate will either be amplified or negated based on what sits beneath it. It's not just about how we look and what we say and how we present. Nor is it about being polished and professional. Nor is it about being raw and messy. It can be any and all of those things and work or not work. It goes way deeper. People are picking up the true *intention* behind what we are doing.

People will sense the energy coming at them beyond what their mind will process and what they see and hear. They feel that deeply, and, are attracted or repelled based on it, and make a subconscious decision about whether or not they want it in their energetic field (you could also think of this as their personal space). It's going to look different if you're a personal brand versus a small business versus a corporate entity, but the principles are the same: **you can't fake an energetic connection.**

When you set out to share something – whether it's on social media, in your content, in an interview, article, or speech, email, wherever – be mindful and check in with the true *intent* and even the *emotion* behind what you're saying. Because sure as anything, that's what your audience is picking up – even more so than what you are actually saying!

Chances are you're feeling something, even if you aren't quite sure how to articulate it, it's just vibing in your bones, and your own personal energetic field. I know this might sound a bit out there, but that's okay. I'm going there because I've tapped into this principle and proven it over and over again, as have countless clients of mine.

Recently I was speaking with someone in his 50's, an accomplished professional who was somewhat confused as to why things weren't working like they used to – when he used to be so good at marketing and sales and attributed his success to having the "gift of the gab". This is a very common conversation these days as people respond to messages and emails less, avoid phone calls, and are harder to reach. Despite the myriad of automations and scalable tools at our disposal, for most professionals building genuine connections is not any easier than it was "back in the day".

As I was sharing a few insights, I started explaining this concept of brand energy, and how it's very real and very relevant to how we communicate and build our audiences these days, and that because of this we need to get better at understanding it. This gentleman is a leading figure in the publishing & media industry and so he got it immediately. It continues to surprise me how people who I would have normally regarded as very "traditional" in their approach to business development, eagerly embrace these principles. Because they have been around long enough to understand the power of connection. And in decades gone, connection was more easily achieved because people didn't have the "blockers" up that they do today, out of necessity.

Just like the polarity of magnets will pull elements into their field, even without physical contact, brand energy will draw the right people into your sphere, as the energetic field that emanates from your brand is allowed to do its work. Our job isn't trying to force connections, rather ensuring the field is clear, unrestricted, and free to do its job of transmitting the intention and emotion from brand to audience.

More than ever **it's about how people feel about you**, your brand, what you do, and what you say. The emotional impact is

more powerful than the cognitive impact. Call it what you like –
the intention, the authenticity, the spirit, the essence.

Brand Energy is something to be aware of and be curious
about. This emerging metaphysical aspect of marketing is set
to change things up in the coming decades in ways we haven't
even though of yet. Personally, I'm excited about watching and
participating in this transition because I feel like we're only
scratching the surface in this area right now. It's set to completely
reinvent the entire approach to business communication.

CHAPTER 4

The Challenges Are Real

I buy socks in bulk and usually the same variety as it's easier for matching. But despite best efforts, odd socks are still very much a thing. I have a box of "sock pairs" kids can dip into as needed – and alongside that, a running "odd sock box" for socks not able to be matched as pairs.

I used to play the "sock matching game" with my younger kids occasionally but now they're older, they're wiser and not at all interested. One day, my kind nanny took it upon herself to take the "odd socks basket" to her place and sort them out.

Later that morning she sent me this picture of her garage floor.

I wouldn't ask for someone to do this. Even for pay. But this little thing saves me and my kids so much mental energy in the morning when it comes time to "put on your socks" as we are getting them out the door for school. Not to mention dodging the occasional tantrum and minimising stress because matching socks can't be found.

There are a lot of things I "could" do to make mornings smoother - but this is a classic example of one simple thing that was right under my nose and very simple, which has been massive for reducing friction and has a big impact on the ultimate outcome I am seeking - in this case, calmer mornings. This is much like a lot of people's personal marketing and business development effort. It's like a box of odd socks, where there is no system built and it's more of a "lucky dip". It has no process to it, but system processes are the things that make your life easier. But it's tough, I get it. The system that worked 12 months ago, or even 6 months ago is unlikely to work today, given the shifts that have happened globally.

When it's your business or brand, sometimes it's hard to see what is that "one thing" that might be keeping you stuck, and the one thing you could do right now, that will make the biggest difference to your personal brand growth. But when you can identify where to direct your focus, energy is more abundant and effort more leveraged. Just solving the odd socks problem makes a huge difference to the emotional climate of mornings in the home!

My expertise, being a mum of five kids, who has run a business alongside that for over 20 years, is being able to cut through and identify the most highly leveraged business development actions.

Firstly, the good news. You already have the essential ingredient – **YOU. ALL OF YOU.**

Whether it's the first or fiftieth time you've thought about building a personal brand, it's worth doing a realistic assessment of what might hold you back or what's been holding you back until now so that you can maximise your chances of building your brand successfully.

There are four areas people struggle most when it comes to their brand. Each one is foundational to the next. These are:

- **Clarity**
- **Confidence**
- **Consistency**
- **Connection**

I'm sure you'll be able to quickly see yourself in one (or more) of these scenarios as we go through them. Nevertheless, agreeing with the need for them, and actually making them happen aren't one and the same. Whether it's healthy eating, committing to regular exercise, or building a savings habit, understanding the need for change and actually implementing it are two fundamentally different things.

We can universally acknowledge the harmful effects of junk food, understand the health benefits of exercise, and appreciate the financial security of savings. Yet, modifying our behaviour can be a significant hurdle. Ingrained habits, the allure of immediate gratification, and everyday disruptions often interfere with good intentions. So too, with building a personal brand.

The stark reality is this: acknowledging the necessity for change is a good starting point, but actual change requires more—it demands actionable planning, a belief in what's possible, overcoming resistance, and embracing your identity. This is the process I am about to walk you through.

What is less obvious though, is that addressing these challenges in the right order will be so much more efficient as each one builds on the last one and makes the next one so much easier. One of the biggest mistakes people make is incorrectly diagnosing their main challenge and expending way too much focus, time, and energy into areas that don't ultimately deliver the business growth and impact they desire.

Depending what stage you are at in your personal brand and business or career growth I can guarantee that subtle tweaks in one or more of these areas can quickly deliver a massive impact on your business and bottom line. This is the case whether you are just starting out building a brand, or are already a seasoned expert seeking to be more widely known. Whether you're an industry leader ready to commercialise their influence, or a global thought leader who is ready to turn more of their audience into clients.

We'll look briefly at each of the challenges here, and why the order is important, then explore the antidote for each of them in future chapters.

Getting Clear

"I need help clarifying my message. I want my content to come more easily because I'm clear on what I have to share that will be relevant and useful to my audience."

If you've ever felt unsure of what to say or how to say it, you're not alone.

Feeling unclear is the easily the biggest hurdle I see, particularly for people in the early stages of building their personal brand – because it's stops so many talented people from getting off the starting blocks. It is also the first thing to address because nothing else really matters if you're not clear on what you want to be known for and how to express it.

So how do you know if you're struggling with clarity?

Clarity is knowing:

- *What to say,*
- *How to say it,*
- *When to say it,*
- *Who to say it to.*

A lot of people think their downfall is not having a system, but there's no use putting in place systems if you don't have clarity on your message, audience and uniqueness. It would be akin to setting up a production line for a food product when you don't have the recipe nailed. You'll just end up producing more content that won't hit the mark. In the best case you'll simply be expending valuable energy – but in the worst case you will put out mixed and messy messaging that will leave your audience confused and not taking action.

Before you start scaling up your content and brand building efforts it's important to be very clear about:

- *Who you are,*
- *What you do,*
- *Who you're serving,*
- *How you can help them,*
- *Why they can trust you.*

Signs you're struggling with clarity could look like asking yourself any of these questions:

- In the realm of infinite possibilities, and with the breadth of experience that you have, what the heck do you talk about?
- What makes you different from everyone else out there doing what you do?
- When you do share personal things, does it even have a point?
- How do you integrate your personal and your business brand?
- How do you position yourself for those speaking gigs and interviews in a way that makes sense for your business or current role?
- Do you find it hard to articulate your value and establish your credibility, because you feel like it might come across as bragging or big-noting yourself?

This usually results in one of three things happening.

- You hold off sharing your message or creating content because you're not sure what to say.
- You share personal things, and people LIKE you – as you mean well, and occasionally share some useful insights, but people still don't know how they can do business with you, and so your effort doesn't feel worthwhile.
- You share random wisdom here and there and demonstrate your competence, but what you share is all over

the place and doesn't attract the right people or lead to commercial conversations.

You might be brilliant but if you're too hard to process you won't connect with your audience. Even if you do connect on a personal level, which is a great start, you can end up attracting the wrong people and the ones who aren't an ideal commercial fit. Whereas when your messaging is clear and dialled in, you draw in people who feel compelled to be in your world and know more about you, because they are clear on how you can help them in their own life or business.

Getting Confident

"There are a ton of people out there who could really use what I have to share, but I suffer from imposter syndrome and a fear of failure."

The first few articles I ever published online I was so scared; I paid a professional copywriter to go over them and fix them up for me. Looking back, the money I spent on editing for each article wasn't about making them better, it was really an investment into my confidence. As someone who had been a professional marketer for 20 years, we'd always used specialists for writing or filming, we were conditioned to think that it had to be at a certain standard. Then along came social media and suddenly everyone had to do it themselves. That took a lot of re-wiring for my brain, which had always felt that I wasn't good enough at these things and didn't want to be seen as anything other than a consummate professional.

I see this time and time again with my *Marketing Me*® clients – from professionals who have never promoted themselves before, through to world-class marketers who have spent their life shining the light on other people: their clients and their employers. Everyone faces the same challenges when it comes to sharing themselves with the world.

A lot of people are clear on *what* they do, and *how* they help people, but they feel awkward about how they are showing up.

Feeling awkward, icky, or impostor syndrome is very normal. Of the countless people I've worked with, only a handful didn't struggle with this. All ages, all levels of experience, all genders, all professions, all parts of the globe. A study by KPMG[6] stated that 75% of women surveyed admitted to experiencing impostor syndrome – and many of those in their day-to-day work. These feelings are massively amplified when you are in the position of sharing yourself with the world to build your personal brand.

Impostor syndrome is one of the most important things a personal brand needs to overcome, because otherwise you show up feeling like you need validation even though you deliver compelling life or business benefits. This is especially true if you're from a culture that frowns upon people 'blowing their own trumpet'.

In Australia & New Zealand it's known as tall poppy syndrome, however it's a global phenomenon. In the USA, which much of the world may characterise as being quite bold and confident, this mindset is often referred to as crab syndrome or "crabs in a bucket" that attempt to pull each other down. The Japanese version is the idea that the nail that sticks out of the wall gets hammered down. And in a recent conversation with one of my African clients she explained that in African cultures, where community and collectivism are often highly valued, standing out can be met with scepticism or criticism. How this can play out differs vastly between different geographies, given the continent's immense diversity in cultures, traditions, and social norms – yet a common result is that there's a perception that meekness is a way to strategically navigate social issues. However, that's often at the expense of stifling individual potential.

Interestingly, in my conversations with First Nations (indigenous) clients, the innate cultural norm is that everyone contributes in different yet equally important ways to serve the collective. Yet the proliferation of the dominant culture of mainstream society has distorted this, and as a result, the mindset of playing small to stay safe has also seeped into the individual perspective. This is something many of my extraordinary First Nations clients are acutely aware of, and they are leading the way by modelling a different way to be.

Whether you're in a country that calls it tall poppy syndrome, crabs in a bucket or a nail sticking out of the wall – whether that's the culture you were born into, or the one that you felt the need to morph and mould to fit into as you grew up, it's something that is a universal challenge of our generation, with fear at the root of it all.

Psychologist Pauline Clance, one half of the duo who coined the term 'impostor syndrome', identified the theory that impostor feelings come from a conviction that people need to mask who they really are.[7]

Nowadays she refers the phenomenon is actually 'an experience rather than a pathology', and makes the point that it's not a diagnosis but an experience that we all have. The masking we do as a way to plug the confidence gap is part of being human.

Writer Leslie Jamison, in her stunning article for the New Yorker, *Why Everyone Feels Like They're Faking It,* talks about the experience as being universal, and more specific than mere self-doubt because it's "a fear of being *found out*" and revealed for who we really are.[8]

This is why there is such emotional charge around authenticity – when it's embraced. Because **authenticity is the metaphorical removal of the mask** that keeps the real us hidden, which **disempowers that impostor phenomenon.**

Even when you know you're really good at what you do, self-doubt can creep in like an unwelcome guest. In my experience, professional marketers tend to experience this as much if not more than anyone. I've even experienced it myself, too!

We see those around us shining bright and think, "Who am I to stand out when there are so many amazing people already doing this?" Not knowing, or truly believing wholeheartedly, that it's our uniqueness that the world needs.

In the background, there is often fear of putting ourselves out there, wondering what people will say. Or being afraid of the judgement, the assumptions, the *"what if it doesn't work"* vibes. Lack of confidence holds so many people back unnecessarily.

With my clients, I often step into the role that the professional writer played for me. I needed another opinion to tell me that what I wanted to share with the world was good enough. Except I don't need to touch what my clients write. It's almost always exceptional, because they've gone through the process of understanding themselves and how to share that authentically with the world. All they need is my encouragement to share it the first time. When they do, inevitably the response blows them away as they are inundated with compliments, support, respect, and quite often, even business leads that come out of the woodwork – all from something that had been sitting within them but that they didn't have the confidence to share with the world.

In my work I used to think success was about skills, expertise, know-how, and commitment and just "feeling the fear and doing it anyway".

Nowadays, I'm convinced that the journey to success as a personal brand is as much about personal development journey as it is about professional development.

Giving someone direction and information, as good as it may be, is not going to get them to their goal if there's no self-confidence. This is an inside job – and it's why I focus on the confidence building side of personal branding, and much less on the tactical side to begin with. Because this is what gets the biggest results the fastest.

It doesn't matter how prolific, smart, or brilliant you are – if you don't feel that your brand reflects the level of the service or knowledge you provide, there is a gap in your confidence.

Confidence comes from the conviction of knowing what you have and do is of value, but it is also important to consider how you're expressing and presenting yourself to the world. As this plays a huge part in how we build our confidence.

It's not enough just to send your message into the world, cross your fingers, and hope for the best, thinking one day this will deliver the confidence you so deeply desire.

Effective marketing messages are ones that are expressed in an elegant way, and the content reflects the quality of the service you provide. A message that resonates with you, is authentic, and also reflects what you have to offer, is sure to resonate strongly with your market.

This makes YOU feel good. And that instils massive confidence.

Getting Consistent

"I can produce something when I need to but my challenge is doing it on a regular basis. I just don't have the time or drive to follow through."

Those business leaders who genuinely have consistency as their major challenge are usually a bit further along in their personal branding journey. I see a lot of people early in their journey mistakenly think they're not further along because they're not "consistent" with their marketing and personal branding efforts.

It's important to note before we get into this point **that if you don't have clarity and confidence – consistency won't help you**. You need to go back and get these sorted out first. But when you do have clarity and confidence – yet are not maximising it, consistency can be a very easy lever to pull that will generate massive business benefit, really fast.

You may have an audience, be well-known, respected for what you do – but perhaps you aren't getting out there often enough to grow your audience and, more importantly, nurture and lead your audience or network through to the next stage of a business relationship with you.

You know that if you had a sustainable, repeatable, simple, and consistent way of getting your message out, your business could be so different. The reason for this is simple. We all have a life, something that fills in the nooks and crannies of our day with lots of legitimate things competing for attention.

For a lot of people, it can be easy to create good content occasionally, but it is much more difficult to do it consistently. When you're motivated, it's a breeze and you're flying, but then life happens. You may fall off the wagon and, before long, you're out of flow. That roll that you were on now has been absorbed by legitimate "business-as-usual" activities. You're in demand and so just don't have the space to add "content creator" into the mix. Or going through the mental gymnastics to think about what to put out on a regular basis.

We're all familiar with the "big rocks" analogy by now, the

lesson where the professor filled the jar with so much more by starting with the rocks, then the pebbles, followed by the sand and finally the water. Putting in place a system for building your personal brand consistently is a "big rock". That said it doesn't have to be "big" time wise or effort wise (in fact I generally recommend it shouldn't' be taking more than an hour a week on an ongoing basis!). But having this in place and operational will take the professional leverage you've built up over the years and turn that into assets that will get your message in front of people with ease and effectively. You will commercialise your position, network and expertise so much quicker.

Getting Connected

"I feel like I don't have anything unique to add to the conversation – how do I stand out in a sea of already well-known people doing amazing things?"

The term "connection" refers to the act of creating a relationship between people, ideas, or objects. Where things are joined together or linked in some way. So, with a personal brand, when "the person IS the brand" it speaks to the relationship that your audience has with you, and what your brand stands for. In this case it's more an emotional than a rational response, as it's less about the physical act of the seeing/reading "about" you. Genuine connection is more about the feeling or desire that is evoked as a result of interacting "with" you.

A lack of connection is probably the most demotivating and depleting frustration in the personal branding process.

You've done the work and you're putting it out there. Consistently, even. You feel like you're in your zone of genius, you're giving your best, and yet it's still not getting through.

This often leaves you feeling flat and questioning whether it's even worth it. This was less of a problem a few years ago, as people consumed more information, but the need to connect to be heard has been amplified significantly in recent years. As the noise has increased, what people are looking for from brands has changed too.

A very common fear I see is people not wanting to add to the noise. There is a deep desire to connect, to make sense, and have meaning with our content but people don't want to "be just another voice in the crowd" as they feel there are already enough people clamouring for attention.

Even if you are clear, confident, and consistent there may be a "dis-**connect**" if people aren't noticing, responding, or taking action.

Generating brand awareness isn't what it used to be. Yes, it's still important, but when it comes to your brand, and moving the needle on the metrics that matter to your business, credibility and connection are the holy grail. I'm reminded of the famous words of ancient scripture "And the greatest of these is love." *If you want to get really deep, genuine connection is the bi-product of love expressed.* So, in the context of building a brand and content marketing, I would adapt this and say, "And the greatest of these is connection."

Even if you've got awareness, authority, and credibility you can easily just be banging a drum and making more noise, regardless of how polished and proficient and professional you are. When you are a personal brand and you truly connect, what you're saying is registering at an emotional level, and even without understanding or being able to rationalise it people are drawn to you so much more.

Connection is an art and a science but there's an element of the quantum-realm infused as well, because the "right" words that come with the "wrong" intention can still land flat. And neither you nor your audience may understand why. It's because it goes beyond intellect and instead goes straight to the heart, making the person feel.

When you amplify your connection factor, it becomes like rocket fuel and has explosive growth on your engagement, responsiveness, and conversion. And regardless of which stage you're at, there are things you can do to amplify your connection and it doesn't have to be elusive.

A big part of this is the identity work that is the main focus of this book, because this is where the power is.

Embracing your identity has more impact on your ability to connect than anything else you could do.

PART II

THE JOURNEY OF THE EMERGING IDENTITY

arketing yourself isn't just about getting your message and expertise in front of more people. At its core it's about people connecting with your authentic identity in a deeper way.

But for that to happen, first and foremost, it's necessary for you to fully embrace who YOU are. Lean into it, and only then, express it publicly.

When you build your brand this way, people don't just notice you, they forge a deep bond and are drawn to you. This creates the "superhighway of connection" so many people are craving right now.

CHAPTER 5

It All Starts With You

"We must overcome the notion that we must be regular... it robs you of the chance to be extraordinary and leads you to the mediocre."
— *Uta Hagen*

These are olden words that are equally true in the arts, in business, and in life. I took these words to heart the first time I read them – ever since I have grown in courage to be less 'regular' and more 'me'. Because, to be honest, to aim to be "fully me" is way less of a stretch than aiming for extraordinary.

It's not always easy, but simply making the decision to be true to yourself steers you out of the "regular zone". Somehow, "regular" so often becomes the benchmark, the comfort zone. Unfortunately doing what everyone else is doing over and over can lead to the slippery slope of blending in, being mediocre or average, and adding to the noise. Putting in effort and still not getting noticed.

People think that being visible is about "showing up".

But the biggest barrier to becoming known is NOT fear of showing up and putting yourself out there. **Becoming known beckons you to embrace, then step into, and then express who you really ARE.** Going on the journey of "finding out who you are becoming" is not for the faint-hearted.

As Marianne Williamson aptly said:[9]

"Our deepest fear is not that we are inadequate. Our deepest fear is that we are powerful beyond measure. It is our light, not our darkness, that most frightens us. We ask ourselves, Who am I to be brilliant, gorgeous, talented, fabulous? Actually, who are you not to be? You are a child of God. Your playing small doesn't serve the world."

I read and heard this quote many times over the years and each time, it sinks in more and more deeply as it becomes my lived experience. I'm still a work in progress, but growing as I go, and definitely embracing the journey.

So, I want to encourage you today,

...if you're motivated to create more impact than you do right now,

...if you feel like there is something in you that you know can powerfully affect the marketplace – or the world,

...but you feel some resistance about getting your message out there, being more visible, and becoming known,

...and you're just not sure why it's not coming together – yet,

....don't be harsh on yourself,

....or think it's just you.

Lean into that desire to have more impact and get excited, be curious, and open to what's coming next. It may just be a sign that you're about to embark on the most amazing and fulfilling journey that is the next chapter of the story of your life.

I'm going to take you through a series of steps shortly. Steps that, when you explore and embody them, are the ones that change how you see yourself, and this has an indelible impact on you as a personal brand, and business.

First, Go Inward

In our ever-changing world, personal transformation is inevitable. As a brand, you will experience periods of growth and change. Amidst all of this, your core identity remains unchanged – that's YOU.

It's important to acknowledge that change will happen. Your marketing strategies when you're a personal brand should align and adjust to your authentic self, rather than forcing you to conform. Instead of constantly reacting to external shifts and trends, let's begin by looking inward.

Understanding yourself is a key to marketing yourself better and is more powerful than any single piece of well-intentioned and sage advice. When you start with the externals and build inward it gets confusing and overwhelming. You end up feeling like a square peg in a round hole, "chasing problems" and trying to cobble together who you want to show up as, to "meet the need".

Simon Sinek became very famous for his book, *Start with Why*, that put purpose at the heart of business decisions and actions. When you're a personal brand "starting with you" has the equivalent potency. Because rather than retrofitting your gifts and abilities, likes and desires, to a perceived problem, you start with the uniqueness and significance of who you are and a deep trust that you were created this way for a purpose. You can then embark on the exciting journey of uncovering how you'll live out this mission.

The Journey of YOU

I used to think I knew pretty much all I needed to know – about myself, the world and life. My confidence through my 20's was strong as I advanced in both the corporate and entrepreneurial world rapidly, full of self-belief and optimism.

Nothing wrong with that. I had good intentions, achieved a lot, and I'm proud of it all.

But it is the classic case of "the more you learn the more you realise you don't know." Looking back, I see clearly that while, outwardly, I projected a confident and together demeanour, a lot of the security I rested in was in the identity I projected as a professional, not in the understanding of who I was as a person.

Fast forward more than a decade, and five children later, I found myself starting to intentionally build a personal brand – in a season of life that led me to questioning the very core of who I am in the world – and to myself.

Outwardly, I looked like I had it all together – and in many ways I did, by most people's benchmark of success relating to juggling parenting and business life, status and freedom. Yet privately, the things that had been the foundations of my identity – who I was to myself, and who I was to the world, were deeply shaken.

I now see what a gift this was, as it led me to embark on a process of going from thinking I know everything about myself, my life and the world (yet having little self-awareness), to truly and deeply understanding who I am. I gained an awareness of how little I actually do know, and quite frankly, am completely unbothered about it all.

I now see very clearly why my attempts in the personal branding space back before this self-awareness emerged were so fraught with resistance. As a professional marketer, I had been so accustomed to following marketing processes and frameworks and practices – I had the tools, the skills and the knowledge – and decades of experience – so I naturally assumed to build my personal brand was just a matter of applying that to myself.

Except it wasn't.

It felt hard, hollow and even harrowing. The real me was hidden. I was trying to be who I thought I needed to be, to fill a mould, fit a role, win the respect of my peers, and it was exhausting. Add to that the pressure I felt as an accomplished and professional marketer to have it all together and it added yet another layer of frustration and self-doubt.

And the irony was, at the time I didn't know that it could be differently.

Figuring out how to market myself led me into an expansive rabbit hole of self-discovery, for which I am extraordinarily grateful for today.

Self-awareness is everything when it comes to this process.

This is book is called "Marketing Me" for a reason. Yet, even with that in mind, I place much less emphasis on the "Marketing..." externals and the role they play in the personal branding process, and so much more on the "...**Me**" side – which sits at the core of a magnetic personal brand.

It's not to say the marketing isn't important. But it's like an oven. You can push the buttons to turn it on, have the trays and racks ready to go, and timers and fanciest of settings, but if there's no heat emanating from the element, you're not going to get that beautiful satisfying meal.

And that's the "Me" in "Marketing Me". When you're a personal brand, that's where the power and potency reside.

Questions to Ask Yourself

To start this journey there are two provocative and expansive questions we need to ask:

WHO ARE YOU – to yourself?
WHO ARE YOU – in the world?

These are not questions with simple answers, but please understand, the power is in the asking, not the answering. The journey to clarity is an ongoing one.

When you get to the place where these two questions co-exist in a beautiful, organic, aligned fashion, the idea of personal branding takes on a whole new meaning. It's no longer about "doing" and "trying" to create – it becomes simply about "being" and this is just so liberating.

A lot of people start with the problem their clients are facing, the services they are delivering and the message they are wanting to share. Instead, we're going to flip that. We will start with YOU, then work outward from there. Consider the other aspects, sure – but as a personal brand the potency of connection will come from knowing yourself deeply, allowing your true self to naturally flourish and emerge, and being open, curious and flexible as you begin the experiment of how you express that genuine self into the world.

"Don't be a Cover Band. Be an original. Be You."
— Nina Christian

In a time when cookie-cutter marketing techniques are shoved in our face every time we jump online, it takes more effort to be unique and original than it does to follow the crowd. But inside you are special gifts to share with the world – ways you can help people, in the way only you can.

It takes courage to be "you" in a sea of noise, rather than attempting to appease the masses for fear of judgement. It takes courage to share an original thought and to be a thought leader. When people choose to follow your leadership through the thoughts you share with the world, that's when your impact starts to skyrocket. Your confidence in your message increases, the momentum begins to build, and you get to impact more people that you really have a heart to serve.

Your message is one of a kind.

Because you are one of a kind.

So "Be YOU" – proudly.

Over several years I developed an effective process based on my own journey, charting the lessons and discoveries that were pivotal in my personal brand development, that I could teach and guide others through. I refined and streamlined these and have seen them work without exception for entrepreneurs, corporate professionals and business leaders of all walks and industries.

My process is unconventional, yet extremely potent, in helping people bust through the clarity and confidence barriers. Let's take a look at the different elements and how they work together.

Journey of the Emerging Identity

In the following chapters we are going to explore each section of this model, and in so doing, get you closer to the two big questions that will define your personal brand:

WHO ARE YOU – to yourself?
WHO ARE YOU – in the world?

Chapter 6
Embracing your Difference

Human nature is wired to desire "new" and "fresh".

There's a sense of inherent optimism that comes with anticipating something different. It's what we look for in brands, and it's what we look for in people too. And this is good news for personal brands, because, just like snowflakes and thumbprints, each one of us brings something different.

Helping people identify and embrace uniqueness is one of the most powerful and eye-opening things I get to do with extremely talented people around the world. Celebrating and then sharing that uniqueness becomes fulfilling and joyful, as it becomes a powerful means of self-expression in the world. When people join my *Marketing Me®* program they often come for the systems, content, and branding methodologies. They are surprised when we spend so much time helping them understand and explore their own uniqueness – I help them join dots they've never realised were there before.

The beautiful thing is you don't have to share everything

with the world; you get to pick and choose. But, when you've got a wider assortment of things to choose from, and you can see how those things can interplay together to support a unique and compelling brand, it is empowering.

The act of articulating and focusing on one's values is extremely powerful and life-changing for so many of my clients, as what is unconscious becomes conscious, and we observe it and how it plays out in not just in their business, but in their life.

Are you specific, clear and observant about your values?

Are you confident in how they are expressed, both personally and professionally?

It's a beautiful circle because once you explore and bring these underlying values to the surface and make them conscious, it's then your mind can "release" them again and again. They go back into the subconscious, but this time with a lens that influences your content, and it results in a subtle but powerful shift in how your content stands out.

"Values are like fingerprints. Nobody's are the same
but you leave 'em all over everything you do."
— Elvis Presley

As well as this inner work, there are also very practical things that you can do that have a big impact.

One of the easiest ways to be different in a 'sea of average', especially in crowded industries, is to tap into what I call your *Power Combo™*. This is where you combine three distinct aspects of your business and personal life, and therein lies the uniqueness.

An easy way to be authentic and memorable is to identify one key element from each of these categories.

- **What you DO**
  (your profession)
- **Who you ARE**
  (one of the hats you wear as a person)
- **Something you LOVE**
  (a passion - anything that lights you up when you talk about it)

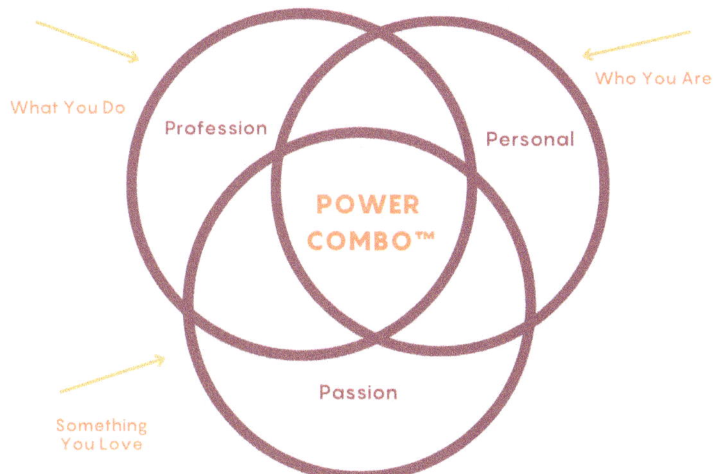

The reason I take this approach is that there are plenty of people doing what you do – whether you're a creative, technology expert, thought leader, leadership expert, service provider or business pioneer. Based on expertise and experience alone you may easily not stand out, but together your *Power Combo*™ creates an awesome story and heightened level of intrigue.

Just like oil, vinegar and egg yolk are fairly standard natural products, when these three elements are combined a new completely substance is formed.

Often the brilliance is in the combination. For example, if you're in the leadership space, people don't just want to hear about leadership strategy and framework. They do want to hear and see in action examples of leadership, and if you are able to weave in stories and perspectives and richness of experience you uniquely bring, and bring it to life with unique and relevant personal examples, and infused you're your passion as you talk about things that matter to you then you will stand out.

Ideally one or two aspects of your *Power Combo*™ are completely unrelated to your work, but then you find a way to relate them and suddenly they are things that coexist. With ease. Writing reflections about these things, people feel like they get to know you. You get to play with it. It comes more easily. It's organic. Often, it's way more visually compelling too!

My own *Power Combo*™ looks something like this.

1. I'm a **professional marketer** (plenty of those, right?).
2. I'm a **hands-on mum** (plenty of those too, right?).

3. I'm an outdoorsy, relaxed, fun, **sporty, nature-loving person** (hello, Instagram influencers aplenty). I'm completely in my element still doing cartwheels and handstands, or sprawled out lying flat on the grass.

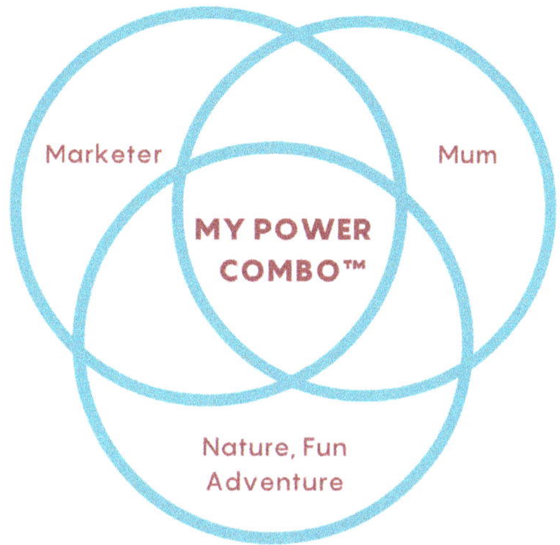

None of those things alone is unique. There are millions in each of those three categories. Yet the combination of those things immediately makes me different. And I've tapped into three things which are aspects of me that are easy to share. There are plenty of others too, just like you have plenty, but I choose to focus predominantly on these three when it comes to my personal brand. For me, it's organic, natural, easy. Together, they make for an interesting combination that sets me apart from other people in that category, when I refer back to them consistently.

This makes content creation easy because if I'm referencing

one of those *power-combo* pieces – either directly or indirectly, it reinforces my brand.

Examples could be:

- I'm talking about marketing while out in nature.
- I'm sharing about a story that happened at a high-profile industry event and you see washing baskets or kids toys in the background.
- I'm wearing sports clothes with kids in tow talking about a business-related principle that feels empowering and relatable to me.

I can slip into the professional space and simply be the author, speaker, and mentor in marketing and branding too – I don't "have to" incorporate those other elements, but a fairly high percentage of my content does infuse other elements into it, and this adds to the relatability, authenticity, and connection factor. Because it's simply reflecting and amplifying who I am.

People feel like they are "in the know" by seeing these snapshots into your life. And you don't need to limit this to social media either, you can talk about them in your speaking gigs, blog posts, emails, website, and images. The key is not having too many elements because then the themes are diluted and you're less memorable and endearing.

There's magic in intentionally weaving in your *Power Combo*™ elements into your master message as you find a story or metaphor that relates to them – which allows you to express what you do, how you do it and why you do it differently in each of those frames. The possibilities are endless, but sometimes endless isn't helpful. So having three "tried and true" lenses to work with and combine with your master message can make the process easier!

The Paradoxical Nature of Unveiling Your Uniqueness

The journey of marketing yourself as an authentic personal brand is full of contrasts and paradoxes. Here's one of my favourites, because both are absolutely true:

You need to find your voice to use your voice.

You use your voice to find your voice.

The two exist together. Simultaneously.

Your voice will be different in 3 months if you are using it continually, as the very use of it will open the pathway for new aspects and depth to come. Knowing you are going to grow and evolve on this journey is important, as well as being ok with that, and starting to use it now.

It's equally important to accept that you don't have to have it all together. You don't have be perfect. That said, you don't have to share your imperfections either. It's not about inciting drama, venting, or trauma dumping. If you don't want public opinion, don't share it – or open it up to public opinion.

Pick and choose, be selective and exercise wisdom around

which bits you share of yourself. This is important because as "personal brands" we are putting our "person" out there for all and sundry. So, we want to be wise about it – and withhold the parts that are deeply personal and precious to us.

Find the Relevancy in Your Legacy

As you think about your professional legacy and your personal history – you can pick out anything you like from that. Think of your history and experiences similar to a library.

Some of them are in the "public" domain, which everyone can access, and borrow and read from. This might be your website, social media, public speeches, or media contribution.

Others are in the "reference" section – where certain people who register and go through a specific process to access what's in them – under certain conditions, in a controlled environment. Perhaps it's your email list, or a closed community, where nothing is certain but it's less likely that that information would be exploited.

Then, finally, there are special books which are off limits. Rare books, historic books, books which have cultural significance. They are purposefully withheld for the purpose of protection and posterity.

It's like that with your brand: you get to pick and choose, and control access.

Be Candid, but Considered

One thing I learned very quickly and have guided many exceptional entrepreneurs and business leaders though, is to ensure that any sharing is not from a place of anguish or hurt – even if the desire is to help others. While the desire for transparency is admirable, there's a big difference between sharing a hiccup or business lesson or frustration and how you've dealt with it, and opening up a deeply sensitive part of your life. That's better saved for therapy.

I see people sharing all sorts of deeply personal things for the purpose of self-promotion, sometimes even gratuitously in advertisements. While there is a time and place for considered vulnerability, inappropriate or over-sharing often leaves the reader with a sense of queasiness and overwhelm rather than endearment. When you are building a brand primarily for commercial purposes it's likely this won't serve your business – or you personally.

A good way to test whether you're ready to share something, is if people were to comment or challenge you about it, would you feel it personally? If it's water off a duck's back and wouldn't bother you, it's probably fine, but if it would make you emotional then I would recommend refraining. **Protecting and managing your emotional state is a key part of being a healthy, whole and vibrant personal brand**, especially if you are primarily doing it for commercial purposes, which is the context of this book.

There is an ancient scripture which talks about not casting your pearls before swine. There are plenty of aspects of my life that I will share, and others I'll intentionally refrain from opening up about – as I don't wish to receive opinions or perspectives on that.

Some years ago, I did wrestle with that, thinking "How will people really know me if I don't share everything?" Because there were certain parts of my life experience that I feel are part of my essence and core; the making of who I am. However, for a variety of reasons, I have zero desire to open up those parts of my life. They remain completely private to me.

For me, the most interesting thing is that I don't even need to share those facets for people to feel the impact of them. I realise this may sound counter-intuitive, but if we go back to the notion of intention and infusing "feelings" into our content, I absolutely believe that people "get what they need to get" via our marketing and content. I witness this time and time again.

Your Position "with a Twist"

We've looked at some simple ways we can we embrace and express our personal uniqueness, now let's look at incorporating "difference" into our *message*.

You might have heard you need to have a controversial or strong point of view to stand out and get noticed. To stand out from the very "meh" content, especially as it's flooded by bots. So, you don't blend into a vague background and feel very same-ish.

And sure, if you've got a polarising perspective (that makes sense) that's great and it'll help you attract the right people quickly. But many people don't know what their point of difference is yet (or may have an inkling but haven't tapped into it fully) – so that idea of trying to come up with something that makes you stand out, makes you want to not share anything.

My alternative to this is what is your "position with a twist" that could flavour everything you do and share, and ease you into embracing your difference. For example, for many years I talked about marketing, branding, content through a very traditional and safe lens of focusing on practical elements like strategy, corporate branding, running an agency, and emerging technology. But I felt my message was very much the same as so many others and probably of a lesser quality than those I respected. Those who frequently shared prolific insights in this space, and had amassed a large global following because of the confidence and insights they exuded.

As I delved more into exploring and embracing my own difference, over a period of about 12 months, a very clear current "position with a twist" started to emerge. As I built my own brand, I became fascinated about sharing what makes people connect with personal brands. And how to build a personal brand people gravitate towards, so you can create more impact. This has morphed into my main message which stems from embracing your identity, and developing a process that helps people do just that (which is what I'm walking you through right now!).

Another "position with a twist" that I embraced was around putting in place robust, efficient, doable systems that help people get their message to more with less effort. So, it goes from hard and overwhelming (which is most people's experience of marketing) to full of ease and energising – which is the way I experience it and how I teach my clients to approach it. Sometimes I'll talk directly about this, and that when you're a personal brand I believe you should have a consistent "one hour a week" marketing strategy – other times it will be subtly infused into whatever I'm sharing about – but it's a constant theme, and one that is by no means polarising, but one that will pique people's curiosity. The "position" is having a repeatable marketing system – the "twist" is to have one that takes you an hour a week.

Sometimes we need to hold back and flesh out our message before we start sharing too. Right now, what lights me up is talking about brand energetics, quantum marketing, synchronicity in content, the art of translating flow moments into brand assets. I could talk about this for days and weeks on end, as I'm still fleshing out the implementable aspects of this. But rather than oversharing, I pepper my content with aspects that are relevant more broadly, and bring people along for the journey, in the way that serves them.

These are examples of how you can explore your "position with a twist" and feed it, and see if it grows. If so, it may well become part of your identity as well. Approach it with curiosity, and allow it to breath, grow and develop. If it doesn't feel like it's breathing and growing that's ok, just set the intention that you want to spotlight another twist and see what comes to you.

Because if you put that intention out, something *will* present itself.

In the end, it all comes down to truly embracing your difference, and your uniqueness. It's about finding that *Power Combo*™ that sets you apart, understanding your core values, and using your voice effectively. It's also about sharing your experiences wisely, and finding that unique 'position with a twist'. Remember, your personal brand is a reflection of who you are, and there's no one else quite like you. So, go ahead, embrace your difference, and let the world see the real, unique you.

Reflection Questions:

1. What makes you unique? How can you embrace and express this uniqueness in your personal brand?

2. What are your core values? How do these values guide your personal and professional actions?

3. What could be your *Power Combo*™? – the unique blend of three aspects of your personal and professional life that sets you apart from others? How can these aspects of your life create a unique narrative for your personal brand?

4. What parts of your history and experiences would you like to share as part of your personal brand? How can you control access to different aspects of your personal brand?

5. How can you share your experiences wisely and considerately, without oversharing or exposing deeply personal or sensitive topics?

6. What could be your "position with a twist" – the unique perspective that you bring to your field, which is slightly different from the norm? How can this "twist" flavour everything you do and share in your personal brand?

Chapter 7
Dialling into Congruence

I was on hold recently with a local medical centre when the all-too-predictable phone message let me know that "At XYZ Medical Centre, we pride ourselves in being a family-friendly clinic." Great, I think, because I'm bringing in three of my kids who all have different things needing attention.

I'm imagining a clinic that can make a block of subsequent appointments with the same doctor, to have clean bathrooms and games and magazines that would appeal to a wider range of ages. One with friendly staff and a comfortable waiting area. What I found was something quite different. When we arrived, it felt the furthest from family-friendly you could imagine: boring medical infomercials on the TV, some rather gory medical pics on the walls for all to see, and not a toy or children's book in sight. There weren't even enough seats for us to all be able to sit in the same area at the same time. Rather than saying you're a family-friendly practice, just DO the things that make it more enjoyable for a child and a parent. It's common sense, for any business really.

The same can be said for a personal brand.

Does this person stack up?

Are they really like what they are presenting to be?

Can I trust them?

These are the questions going on in the mind of your audience, all the time. **If there is congruency around your brand it makes you believable.**

Communicating your values is imperative, but don't TELL people what you stand for, SHOW them! "*We pride ourselves in...*" has no place in modern marketing. It reeks of 1995. People have been conditioned to filter out mundane marketing-speak; the words are meaningless.

The big thing about congruence is that it operates in the unseen realm, there are rarely "fact checkers" out there, it's simply a feeling people get.

In the past a public persona could be faked. And sometimes they still are. But the difference now is that people's extra-sensory perception has been dramatically heightened. Their ability to differentiate what's real and what's BS is finely tuned. It's a big part of what's "felt" – and so no longer can you just "say" something and expect people to take it as gospel.

Five years ago, I was stopped in my tracks by this sign as I hurried to a meeting in the city. I recall the seemingly inconsequential act of grabbing the phone, snapping the pic and crafting a quick caption for social media. It was along the lines of how our actions speak louder than our words. Little did I know what was to follow...

The moment was short, and I didn't know it at the time, but the impact ran deep. Being in the early stages of building my public profile as a personal brand, I couldn't shake the thought on this sign, it stayed with me for weeks. In fact, it was instrumental in setting me on a new path which led me to the space I'm in today. Years later, it feels even more potent today than it felt back then.

The need for alignment across thoughts, words and actions, at every level, both for business brands and personal brands, is essential. If you commit to a cause, fly a flag or jump on a bandwagon, great – but people are carefully watching to see how you act, treat people, and if your actions match what you say. If you say you stand for something, people are watching carefully to see how your actions stack up and if they are genuine. If not, people will pick it up.

Why People Click with Congruency

I often share pictures of myself in nature – simply because I spend a lot of time in nature. It's not staged, it's real. In my blogs and emails, I talk a lot about how I schedule "thinking time" and space to just "be" into my work week. I have found this "thinking time" to be my personal superpower, so I'm a big advocate of it. I do it often, usually weekly at least, sometimes multiple times a week. It's uplevelled my potency and ability to have massive impact, more than any other single thing.

And so, I share it, in order to help others experience the power I've found through it. Hence, the pictures. My strategic thinking is usually done outdoors so that's why there are images of me by rivers, on grass, near trees, by the ocean, or on mountains, most of the time with no make-up and in sports clothes.

Supporting the message with images adds to the connection factor of the message. If people only ever saw me in an office or café or corporate events that wouldn't have the same impact. Conversely, if I were sharing pictures of myself in nature and it was "staged" for the purpose of my social media feeds, rather than capturing me "in the wild", it may look nice, but there is the unseen, unexplainable congruency factor at work in the background. It would undermine the connection factor of those images, regardless of how impressive they were.

On the following pages are some examples of some of my actual social media posts. This first one was taken just behind my house, as I went for a walk to decompress my brain, moments after I'd delivered an online masterclass.

The graphic over the page is a reflection of my *Power Combo*™ – marketer, mum and outdoorsy fun. I was travelling with my girls in Tasmania on a business-related trip, and we had some downtime on the beach with one of my business friends and her daughters. The handstand wasn't done "for" the photo – I just couldn't help myself, and so started a handstand competition for the four girls and captured the moment. And of course, taking a road trip with my kids needs no explanation. This is a visual representation of my *Power Combo*™ and adds to the connection people feel with me, more so than if I were only showing the polished and professional side of what I do.

Everyone has multiple "sides" and there's no single side that is inherently right or wrong, or less important or valuable than another. It comes down to the spirit and intention that sits behind it, and how you use it, that determines how it comes across. For example, as a mum and outdoors enthusiast, 80% of my time is spent in casual wear. Very occasionally, I'll dress up for a special event – and maybe once or twice a week I'll do my hair and make up for work, or if I'm speaking at an event or running a workshop and want to present professionally. Both personas are still me, but I make no secret that the majority of my work time is not looking polished and professional. I choose to let people see me with messy hair and frequently with no makeup. That's not for everyone, of course, but I've made the strategic decision that I'm comfortable bringing that into my brand.

There are lots of ways to show your personality beyond your work life – and I see people do those really well – especially if they love cooking, art or are heavily involved in their children's sports. Perhaps their jam is shopping or getting glammed up. I can guarantee that if there was a picture of me blowing confetti in a bubble bath, or of me with my kids all dressed in pristine white linen, those images might look great and get some temporary interest, but wouldn't have the same overall impact on my brand, because it's not congruent with what I actually do in my everyday life.

This is an important point and where the personal brand has a big advantage – but it's also where a lot of people miss it. If it's not authentic, people will pick it up. There are a lot of "influencers" who go to great lengths to curate that perfect nature shot. I've heard stories of people driving hours, setting up all the equipment to get that "perfect shot" then immediately packing up and going home. It might be a very beautiful shot, and get a great response and engagement, but when it comes to the trust and congruency factor, it's something that audiences are more and more perceptive about.

When you see people posing in front of a private jet that you know they've just driven out to the airport to take pictures with, you may not be able to put your finger on it, but those images repulse you. Even if you don't know the facts. It's not the jet, it's the authenticity. Because if you saw Richard Branson or Beyoncé in front of a jet it would absolutely be congruent.

If you try to front something that's not who you really are, audiences these days can sense it, and will tune out, even if they're not sure why.

The Visual Connection

I'm not saying don't try and take a nice image, of course. Let's face it, if you're actively building a personal brand for commercial purposes, it's most likely that there will be some visual expression of that and most of the time that includes images. There are people who use an avatar or single image on repeat – in some cases even a pseudonym, but that's a much harder and longer way to build connection into your personal brand. And while I do find the notion of sharing pictures of myself a little outside my comfort zone, I know it's helpful to my audience, my brand and my long-term strategy so I'm open to doing it, in a way that I feel comfortable.

I have found that when you are a "personal brand" having pictures of yourself in multiple contexts – especially relating to your *Power Combo*™ – can be a huge asset that can accelerate and deepen the connection your audience feels with you.

Part of having confidence in your personal brand is also being happy with how your brand is being expressed, and if it takes a few snaps to get that right, there's nothing wrong with that. To be fair, when it comes to things like lighting and angles, it's something you get better with as you practice. Just like the ability to identify the "moments" and memories that will best serve your brand.

Capturing "moments that matter" is a brilliant way to build your brand – and your network – as I discovered a few weeks ago. I'd arranged to meet up with an industry colleague from Perth, and he asked if he could bring a few mates along. I didn't get to chat with everyone, but I did get into a nice conversation with someone who asked how I had gotten to know my colleague, and who was curious about my work and my book. We had a lovely conversation, and as he left he asked if we could take a selfie, saying he does this with everyone he connects with. Shortly after this image landed in my DMs.

I'm very familiar with the concept and practice of selfies, I routinely take them, especially with others, but what impressed me was the smoothness, and speed at which the interaction took place. So automatically, and it felt so natural and fun. When I received the selfie afterwards I discovered that I'd been speaking to TikTok Influencer Seva Mozhaev, who has amassed 1.6 million followers through his ability to build connection and as a creator.

We had a beautiful messaging exchange during which I remarked on the selfie interaction we'd had. To which, he made this comment, which I thought was particularly profound.

"Selfies are a moment captured in time that become a ticket to return back to. A time capsule, to commemorate the significance of a friendship, partnership, or even simply a meeting of meaningful significance."

Just like Seva, who now has 1.6m followers, did this with such adeptness, it was a reminder to me that integrating our marketing with our life is so much easier when it's "habitualised" and "normalised" rather than something you have to "go out and do".

"Selfies are a moment captured in time that become a ticket to return back to."
— Seva Mozhaev, TikTok Creator

The ability to "think in content" is a core principle of what I teach in my *Marketing Me*® programs, because that instils in us the ability to live our everyday life, and identify those moments that we can draw on that will support our business message – especially when these sit within our *Power Combo*™. The example below is another personal one that illustrates how we can share parts of us, in a way that feels good to us and those around us.

Despite the fact that I'm personally very active as a professional personal brand on social media, most of my children prefer to maintain their privacy and not be part of my public photos. They are fine with us taking photos together for my personal use, but some of them prefer I don't post them publicly. I have a close relationship with all of my children and totally respect and admire their choices.

So, for me this presents an opportunity to think creatively about how I communicate my power combo – particularly the "mum element" in a respectful way. When I can, I will take my children on a business trip – which is often a brilliant time to share interesting images and content. On this occasion I travelled with my daughter who at the time preferred not to be identifiable in the images.

In this instance, I created a post about how this trip with my daughter reminded me of how much I've learned over the years while parenting five children and running a business – and shared 10 powerful lessons – one of which was respecting my children's need for privacy! I got to tap into my *Power Combo*™, be authentic, while also sharing insights that will help others – and align with my brand and business.

This *Power Combo*™ expression in this post sparked lots of interesting conversations both on LinkedIn and beyond in my community, in emails, and in my workshops. And I honestly believe this "worked" and had this impact not just because of the content alone, but because of the heart and intentionality that sat behind it, where this post was an accurate reflection of what happened in our lives, not a curated presentation for social media.

I don't generally share too much personal information publicly because that doesn't feel good to me – I'll generally stick to my *Power Combo*™ elements, and am pretty transparent about those areas – because I know that is in service to my audience. I actively keep my eyes open for opportunities to share every-day occurrences that I believe have a message or will help people. And not just on social media – I'll share these in my emails, blog, videos and trainings.

I'll also share interactions and stories that unfold with my clients too, often they get to see even more of the "behind the scenes" that goes on, which inspires and empowers them. And this why a lot of them will share my content publicly. I believe it has a lot to do with the congruency factor – what you see and experience of me inside my programs is the same as what you see outside, which is the same as who I am with my friends, family and in professional settings, too. The congruency factor isn't something we craft and create – it simply exists (or not) and it seeps through, not just in our content, but in everything that we do.

If I didn't intertwine the personal with the professional, my message would not be as relatable and empowering. And I do have a lot of good stuff to share professionally and also life experience that I know really helps people. Because of this, I make a concerted effort to deliver useful insights in all my content and support it by sharing parts of my life (predominantly from my *Power Combo*™) that serve as connection points both to me and to my message.

Being Yourself is So Freeing!

We live in a phenomenal time, when thankfully, being ourselves is the new normal. While there are definitely fresh challenges that face young people, that people of my age didn't have to face entering the workforce, I'm so grateful that the next generation are growing up knowing it's ok to be the fully-expressed version of them, rather than having to fit a certain mould to be successful.

I'm inspired by so many young adults embracing this way of living, working and being at a far younger age than me and many of my peers. Ironically, so many of us have to unlearn decades of instilled behaviours around this, but this is such an opportunity! And so freeing, compared to how things used to be – not just for your personal brand, but for you as a "person"!

Not too long ago, I had the pleasure of delivering a workshop on personal branding to one of the marketing teams at Atlassian. I recalled to this group of young marketers how hard my younger self once tried to look older just to be taken seriously. I would represent my company (an international sports marketing agency) at meetings with C-suite executives from companies like Bayer, Bosch, DaimlerChrysler, Fujitsu and Siemens and was managing a team older than me. I was appointed General Manager of the company at the very fresh age of 25, and to be taken seriously I remember going to the hairdresser asking for an "old lady hairstyle". I wore lots of pearl necklaces and earrings, and carried a heavy leather briefcase.

I can't believe I used to dress like this, I used to feel so awkward, but I did it anyway. It was anything other than the authentic me. I was most at home in sports clothes and street wear. I didn't like wearing pearls, and short coiffed hair – but I felt like I had to put on a persona to be respected and accepted. I smiled as I recounted these very different days back in the 90's to the talented young marketers from Atlassian at my personal branding workshop because it's a *very* different ballgame these days.

Today we have complete freedom to embrace our uniqueness, our personality, and be ourselves. Thankfully.

Embracing the Authentic "Brand You"

The reality is that you already HAVE a personal brand – whether you like it or not, regardless of what profession you're in. The more relevant point is: How much are you going to embrace it, influence it, and leverage it?

Your personal brand is way more than your appearance. A quote I love about branding often attributed to Jeff Bezos is, "Your personal brand is what people say about you when you're not in the room." Definitely true. But I like to add something to this: I believe that **your personal brand is what GETS you in the room!**

The business leader who invited me to speak at Atlassian remarked that it was my personal brand that prompted us to connect, and that led to me presenting to the team. But it doesn't just happen, you need to be intentional about it. You need to be authentic and real, or else you won't connect, no matter how smart or cool or polished you are.

As you embrace your true identity, then express it, you have way more impact. And why this is so powerful because it's a far more authentic and stress-free way to do marketing when you're a personal brand. And when you do it congruently, it's not just more effective, it's also way more sustainable which means you can do it for longer without feeling like it's taking over your life.

Throughout this chapter, we've explored the importance of congruence in personal branding. We've seen how it operates in the unseen realm, influencing people's perceptions and trust and how it's about aligning our actions with our words, and ensuring that our public persona matches our private self. Being true to who we are, and letting that authenticity shine through in everything we do, by "showing", not telling, our values and what we stand for.

We've also looked at how sharing authentic images and

stories that reflect our everyday life can strengthen our personal brand and deepen the connection with our audience. We looked at how freedom and empowerment comes from embracing your authentic self and expressing that in our personal brand.

Remember, your personal brand is not just about what people say about you when you're not in the room. It's also about what gets you in the room.

Embrace your true identity, express it authentically, and watch your impact grow.

Reflection Questions:

1. How congruent is your personal brand? Are your actions in alignment with your words and values?

2. Are there areas where you could be more authentic in your personal brand? Are there aspects of your life or personality that you could share more openly?

3. How can you show, not tell, your values and what you stand for?

Chapter 8
Expressing with Elegance

When you are clear on the difference and uniqueness inherent in your brand and your message, and have the congruency factor dialled in, the next place to direct your attention is on how you express that elegantly.

Elegance in the personal brand context, isn't talking about being the Audrey Hepburn or Grace Kelly of your industry. According to the Oxford Language dictionary, elegance is *"the quality of being graceful and stylish in appearance or manner; **pleasingly ingenious and simple"**.*

More than just a brand looking pleasing and evoking good vibes, the simplicity aspect is integral for commercial success.

People's ability to absorb information is at an all-time low, and that includes people for whom your product or service might be the perfect fit for their needs. Many have mentally "checked out" for a host of legitimate reasons, so we can't expect them to put in the effort to wade through truckloads of content and strain their brain trying to work out what you do, who you do it for, and how you can help them.

Many business leaders and experts who are actively trying to elevate their personal brand and public profile are tempted to share great volumes of thought leadership on a vast array of topics. The result is that they're all over the place. Random this, random that, we see them pop up here, there, and everywhere, yet we need to be Sherlock Holmes to work out what they actually do! In the words of Donald Miller, "if you confuse, you lose".

"If you Confuse, you Lose"
— Donald Miller, Author, *Building a StoryBrand*

Elegance is achieved through a well-thought through mix of brand clarity, visual cohesiveness, and messaging potency. The ability to be able to hold information back, restrain and curate which ideas you share and when, and not vomit your knowledge everywhere, is sheer elegance in action. For many experts and thought leaders, dialling back the volume of the information they're putting out, is hard – as there is a subtle but compelling desire to constantly share something different.

One of the things I love is working with founders and leaders in organisations that do complex, clever "hard to explain" things – think technology, health, legal, infrastructure, finance and heck, even marketing – where there are so many facets of their knowledge and expertise. Showing them how to sift through the volume of ideas and messages and get clear on what is going to most connect with their audience becomes so liberating. It saves so much mental angst from going around in circles, second guessing their content, and best of all, the power of their platform increases quickly too.

It takes discipline, but talking about one thing long enough and consistently enough allows people to absorb it over a period of time. So that even if they're scanning or glancing at you or your work occasionally, they "get it". A sturdy set of messaging guardrails can help you stay on message.

If you have trouble expressing yourself clearly and elegantly –you're in good company – almost everyone feels the same. Marketers are no different. I find it fascinating that a lot of marketers find it easy to help their clients, but get all up in their heads when it comes to their own messaging and positioning.

Being able to be elegant in the way you turn up as a brand is like the golden goose of marketing skills – it's the gift that keeps on giving! And the good news is that while it doesn't come naturally to most of us, anyone can learn it!

Brevity - Beautiful and Refreshing

Being succinct and concise doesn't restrict you to short writings; it's about clarity and efficiency. You have this book in your hands or on your screen, and while it's not a brief piece, it could have been much longer. In the interest of making it an easy read, I've kept it to a minimum.

It was so important for me to constantly keep in focus the central "one big idea" of this book which is that it's your identity that powers your impact. This ensures that every word in the book supports that purpose, helping readers understand and absorb it better.

The most difficult thing that I experienced while writing this was having to leave lots of great thoughts on the shelf, for now. Not because it's not great information. Not even because it won't help people. But because too many insights, too many thoughts and ideas will make it hard to absorb and confuse the main, big idea of the book.

We can be known for lots of things, but not lots of things at once. People these days are looking for specialists. People who are the best in the field in what they do. Yet at the same time craving simplicity and short-cuts.

We need to make it easy for people to understand us. And easy for them to recognise us, to capitalise on the memorability and connection factor.

Beyond that, we need to be easy to engage with and transact with.

People these days will do their own desktop research before they contact you. They'll look at what you publish and what others are saying about you, before making a decision on whether you're the right person or organisation to help them.

If you're sharing too many ideas in different directions, too many services and offers – you're making it hard for people to know who you are and what you do. If your brand isn't visually cohesive, you miss exposure opportunities to be front of mind, and reinforce your position as a premium brand. **Make life easy for your future clients by being super clear and succinct with what you're communicating**, eliminating the clutter, having consistency across your brand expression, and ensuring you don't have mixed messages.

When creating content, it's always useful to imagine that there are two types of people in your audience – the "scanners" and the "deep-divers". The scanners can glance at your work, quickly recognise that it's you, and get a sense of what you're about. The deep-divers want to engage in a more focused way. Give them opportunities to go into more detail, while resisting the temptation to introduce too many themes and directions into your work. Depending on context, we all consume content in one of these two ways. You can appeal to both by employing the strategic use of headings, graphics, short-form content and multimedia.

One of the most important things I focus on, with everyone who works with me – whether as a private client, as a team in a corporation, or in one of my public programs, is that the strategy and messaging is very clear and visible on one page. When you're a personal brand, anything more than that means it's too long and it doesn't get actioned.

Tough as it might feel, **you need to get clear on what the ONE THING is you want to be known for and easily referrable for.** It might not land for you immediately, that's ok. Just put out the intention that you're seeking that clarity, and it will come eventually. Then unleash your creativity in finding different ways to talk about that same thing. Different stories, metaphors, and perspectives. Fresh and unconventional ways to communicate your core principles.

But all leading back to the ONE THING that you want to be known for right now.

That's being in service to your audience.

It's beautiful and elegant.

Be More Butterfly

It was a warm sunny day and I was out for my morning walk. I am blessed to live by a beautiful stream with preserved native wetlands, teeming with wildlife. I often retreat there during breaks, and to bookend my workday before I shift my focus to parenting.

On this particular day, I was walking as usual, when a couple of flies came buzzing around my face. I wanted to enjoy the scenery, but no matter how hard I swished and swatted my hands around, sighed and snorted, they were relentless, persistently targeting my nose and my mouth. Finally, they found something more interesting and thankfully left. Greatly relieved, I resumed my walk.

I was gazing at the cool blue water when some movement on the other side of the path suddenly caught my eye. It was a beautiful, fluttering butterfly.

Mesmerised, I stopped in my tracks to watch. It landed on a shrub and rested for a moment. Then it spread its colourful wings, and danced in the air before descending on another bush. Its beauty was compelling and I couldn't take my eyes off it, I even stopped my walk to get closer and just admire it.

This was in stark contrast to the flies that were intent on annoying me just minutes earlier. Both insects, both unexpected, but a totally different experience. And it reminded me of marketing; especially content.

This perfectly articulated why we are repelled by some brands and attracted to others.

Many people market themselves like flies – being annoying and shoving themselves into people's faces (feeds, inbox) with no differentiation, creativity, or uniqueness. Maybe even getting a clever "bot" to write their content or using persistent, thoughtless techniques to get right in people's faces in order to get noticed. They act like bothersome pests and this makes us want to run a million miles in the opposite direction.

Then, other people create things that are beautiful and these things attract, and even mesmerise people. It might not be quite as much as they'd like to, but when they do show up, they attract attention for the right reasons. Their brand and content is unique, thoughtful, elegant. A thing of beauty. Drawing a person's gaze away from their regular, day-to-day business as they stop for a moment and admire and absorb.

This doesn't happen just because of the aesthetics, but also the movement, the experience, the thoughtfulness, and the underlying message. They become a highlight, something that makes people's day better. Just like this butterfly did on my walk.

I believe the world needs more butterflies, especially right now, as we are done with being bombarded by cookie-cutter "same-same" messages and marketing approaches.

You could say my *Marketing Me*® praxis is a bit like "butterfly school". It's for caterpillars, for those in the chrysalis, or for butterflies who need an audience. Tapping into the essence of what makes you unique and beautiful, and turning that into compelling marketing content that enriches people's lives that gets attention because it's attractive and authentic, and then expressing that elegantly, beautifully. This results in drawing the right people into your world, building connection, respect, and admiration among those who are ready to benefit from what it is that you do. In an information-saturated world, this is where the opportunity is.

Be less fly.

Be more butterfly.

In a world overflowing with information and choices, elegance in personal branding involves more than just creating a visually pleasing presence. It's about distilling your uniqueness, curating your ideas, and delivering your message and value proposition in a graceful and impactful manner.

In a world where potential clients research extensively before reaching out, clarity is your ally and the key to attracting and maintaining attention. Get clear on the "one thing" you want to be known for and find creative ways to convey it while maintaining consistency. The elegance of your brand expression and the cohesion of your message contribute to your memorability and connection factor.

True elegance arises from the strategic fusion of brand clarity, visual coherence, and impactful messaging. The ability to hold back information, knowing what to share and when, is an art in itself. Often restraint is the very essence of elegance, enhancing the beauty power of your platform by enabling better absorption of your message over time.

Elegance that Energises

There is an intriguing side effect from getting your messaging dialled in and nailing your branding that may surprise you. It's the impact it has on YOU, and how you FEEL about yourself, and your business.

Time and time again I see people follow the process I've outlined in this book for identifying their uniqueness, crafting their congruent brand and refining their messaging, and after the first few years I was astounded at this one thing. They emerged from this process with a new love and enthusiasm for what they do. They would talk about feeling "alive" and "energised" in their business.

This is a whole new area. This whole mojo stuff. And to be honest, it did take me by surprise because it wasn't what I was expecting. I experienced it myself when I went through this process – because there's a real joy that comes with being able to express the authentic you with the world. But here's the thing. It's moved out of the realm of woo, to a modern marketing necessity. Having energetic connection with your audience is what will draw them. Elegance in your communication is what makes it commercially worthwhile.

Making the connection between your business and the very core of who you are, what your business stands for, and why you exist – infused implicitly and elegantly into all your messages, in lots of different ways. People pick up what they need from you, without you having to "say" it. There's both art and the science behind this approach. And freaking heck, it's so powerful.

Which is why I'm more passionate about personal branding than any other aspect of marketing right now. It's helping people who are good at what they do, and passionate about making an impact, do that with greater energy, efficiency and ease. This is exciting because it has a direct correlation with the next stage we're going to look at.

Reflection Questions:

1. Am I overwhelming my audience with too much content and information?

2. How can I simplify my messaging to make it more accessible to my audience?

3. What is my "one thing" that I want to be known for right now?

4. What strategies can I implement to ensure consistency and cohesion across my brand?

5. Are there ways I could be more creative in reinforcing the "one thing" I want to be known for?

6. How can I balance catering to both scanners and deep-divers in my content?

7. What steps can I take to be more elegant in my personal branding, both in appearance and communication?

Chapter 9
Stepping into Confidence

Confidence is "a feeling or belief that you can do something well or succeed at something". It's a deep belief in yourself, and your abilities – and the willingness to act accordingly.

Confidence as a personal brand doesn't come purely through **knowing what you know**, but by **knowing who you are,** understanding **how you know what you know,** and **what to do with what you know.**

When you have confidence, you stop second guessing yourself at each turn. You're ok stepping into bigger opportunities, taking more risks, and feeling good about what you create along the way – with less attachment to the outcome and external validation. Because your belief comes from the inside. A belief in yourself over the response or actions of others.

Building Belief in YOU

A powerful revelation came through a conversation with my 8-year-old son last summer while we were away camping at a favourite spot.

One of the regular camp activities we do is the "leap of faith" – which involves climbing up to a platform that sits atop a 10m high pole with a harness, helmet and rope attached. The other end of the rope is held by a professional instructor, and as the climber leaps off the platform, the tension of the rope and speed of descent is controlled by the instructor who gently lowers them to the ground.

We had done that activity in the morning, and in the after-noon, made our way down to the river for a spot of canoeing and swimming. My 10-year-old daughter spotted a footbridge that spanned the river where some teenagers were jumping off into the water, and decided she wanted to try it.

My son, not quite the confident swimmer my daughter is, made an insightful comment. Walking along, observing the bridge, he said *"it's like a leap of faith, but with water underneath. So basically, it's a Leap of Confidence, because confidence is having faith in yourself."*

"With the leap of faith", he continued, *"you have courage to jump because you trust in the rope and the person pulling you down. But with the Leap of Confidence, you have the courage to jump into deep water because you trust in YOUR ability to swim in deep water."*

This revelation had a powerful impact on me personally – not just because it came through my son, but because it spoke to me about the importance of belief in ourselves, not just in all the external things we put our trust in.

When you're a personal brand, having that level of trust in your own ability is everything. Knowing you can take that leap of confidence because you've got what it takes, even when you land in deep water.

Confidence is not something you "try to have" or talk up, even if you repeat a mantra enough times. It's something that's deep-seated and infused into everything you say and do. Just like when herbs are infused into an oil and become "one" with the oil, flavouring whatever food that oil touches, the confidence of the brand exudes in every expression of the brand. It doesn't mean you don't get nervous, have scary thoughts or make mistakes. That happens to all of us, regardless of where on the confidence spectrum we are. And that's ok. Confidence is a work in progress regardless of who you are.

While there's no magic pill for confidence, following the process I have walked you through in the previous chapters *will* lead you to a place of strong belief in yourself – and in the ***uniqueness and significance*** you bring to the world. Even more so when there's the clarity around how to express that in an elegant way that makes commercial sense to your overall purpose. This is why I spend the majority of my time with clients in these three areas, way more than the marketing systems, tools and activities they do to spread their message. There is so much more efficiency and leverage around all of these external things when the inner foundations of the brand are in place and the confidence is growing.

This flies in the face of lots of marketing gurus who say you just need to show up more to get visible – if you have no idea what to say, or how to say it, it can leave you feeling awkward and exposed and wanting to run for cover, and negatively impact your confidence which hinders your growth.

The first video I ever created for my personal brand, I did it on the armchair in my bedroom, and spent probably an hour recording and re-recording a 5 minute video. I was just embarking on building my brand after having my fifth child, and didn't have the process I now do, which is what I'm sharing in this book. I wasn't clear on who I was, what I was saying or even why I was doing it, to be honest, apart from doing what I had seen other personal brands do. It was awkward, stilted and felt totally ick. My confidence factor was probably 5%. It went onto my Facebook account for a few hours, before it was trolled – someone made a nasty and sarcastic comment – within an hour of me posting my first ever video, and of course, I immediately took it down.

So much for putting myself out there. That was such a negative experience, and it was at least a year before I had the courage to try again. I still pat myself on the back for taking action, but had I had access to the principles I share in this book it absolutely would have had a different outcome.

I now follow the process I've shared with you, and as I embarked on sharing content with these foundations in place, to my knowledge in the many years since I don't recall a negative comment, much less a nasty and sarcastic one like my first video elicited. It's not to say I never will, and if people choose to do that, then of course that's about them, and not about us. The important thing is that I'm not primarily focused on the external responses. What I do know is my confidence is in such a different place now, and that reflects in the way I connect with my audience and comes across through the content I share.

This is also what I have observed working with and mentoring countless clients in this space – it's not about the expertise and knowledge – they have that before they find me. It's not about knowledge of the tools and platforms – anyone can research or google that. These aren't the things that determine the growth of the brand. The big shift is their confidence, hands-down, and I watch them start to see how unique and amazing they are, and how to translate that into their brand. Embracing this processing and baby-stepping your way into expressing that, you will find that what you do share is a lot better received (because it's authentic, congruent and aspirational). When I see clients experience this, their confidence is immediately buoyed and they become far more visible and influential with less physical effort and moreover, less emotional angst.

When you are the personal brand – you're the product they're engaging with, you're the face people are connecting with, you're the reputation they are attaching to.

The confidence that will power personal brand growth comes through knowing:

- *Who YOU are,*
- *Why what you're sharing MATTERS, and*
- *How to do that in a way that is easy and FEELS GOOD.*

This is hands down the fastest way to build that internal belief as a personal brand.

It sounds basic but so many people miss it. People think it's all about understanding the audience or the technical knowledge and sure, that plays a role– but it's just a small part. Understanding and embracing YOU will make you stand out, be attractive, and exude confidence. This is the magic trifecta.

A lot of popular personal branding advice encourages you to just wing it and put stuff out and show your expertise. The #1 difference between people who market themselves well and those who don't is *not* their expertise, marketing know-how, or even determination. Nope, without a doubt it's self-confidence.

I mentor countless experts around the globe who are world-class in their area of expertise, yet still struggle with the "am I good enough/ special enough?" feels. I'm talking about amazing legal powerhouses, global leaders in the tech, finance sectors, and even renowned international figures in the wellness industry and mental health space. And not only professional services experts, I also mentor countless marketing specialists with decades of experience doing marketing for their clients or employer, yet they feel paralysed when it comes to marketing themselves.

It's part of being human. And I can tell you emphatically it does NOT come naturally. Self-confidence around marketing is something we all have to build when we are a personal brand. It takes time – and gentleness with ourselves – but there is a way you can build it quickly, following the pathway I'm outlining here – which is based on understanding your **difference,** being **congruent**, expressing yourself **elegantly.** These are the foundational pillars to personal branding with confidence. When you get this locked in the rest of the details just fall into place effortlessly.

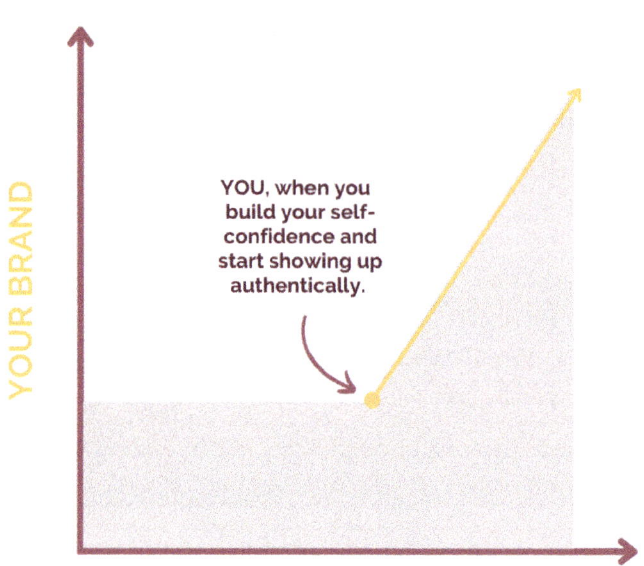

From Awkward to Authentic: How to Be More Confident Showing Up

I can tell you from personal experience that even after years of creating personal brand content, the mind gremlins still come. This isn't a sign of inadequacy; it's part of the human experience. But it also becomes a whole lot more personally energising and rewarding, when you plug into how to do it **authentically.**

And from the place of putting your message out as a gift to the world, rather than something to be measured and meticulously monitored. Now, I put things out and really don't care at all what the response is. Because I know there was one person that needed to read that and this is motivation enough. On top of that, it becomes way more effective commercially, for your business or career when you know how to do it **strategically**.

You don't have to have it "all-together" before you start creating content. But you do have to start. The principles I've outlined in this chapter will help you do it in a strategic and authentic way to find your voice, get the clarity you need, and build your self-confidence around getting your message out there.

Your Confidence is What the World Needs

On the day I was finishing this chapter I had a profound conversation with my oldest son, while driving to an appointment. We were just discussing daily life – school, sport, and somehow, we got talking about confidence. Because I believe in the synchronous nature of conversations my curiosity was piqued, I was all ears, especially as I had been reflecting so deeply on the whole area of confidence and personal brands all that week.

Our conversation centred around how that there is a positive spectrum and a negative spectrum where at one end, people confuse confidence and egotism, and at the other end, they confuse humility and self-doubt. His lens (because he brought up the whole conversation) was his personal development and growth and how he worked on different areas of his life. My lens was how it translated to marketing yourself as a personal brand. Of course!

Listening to so many people's innermost fears on the topic through the work I do, I know a lot of people are scared to put themselves out there either fearing they will be judged as egotistical (or possibly even become that, and this scares them even more). There are plenty of people who are putting themselves out there as self-proclaimed experts or leaders trying to present as confident, but there's a sense of ickiness about it. They might say and do the right things, but because they aren't in full conviction and confidence about it, we pick that up as well, even if we can't always put our finger on why. We just know it doesn't have the authenticity factor. And that affects how people perceive them and their message. If it feels icky to them, it feels icky to people on the other end of that.

The reality is, you can be confident in your abilities and still be humble – not thinking you're better than others, and still willing to learn and improve.

People are looking for leaders with confidence – with substance. Where there's genuine belief in themselves, and moreover genuine belief in their ability to help or deliver outcomes for others.

It doesn't serve your audience, the world, or yourself to hold back your brilliance. To diminish your abilities, or downplay your belief in yourself.

If you believe that playing small, questioning your abilities and entertaining self-doubt is being humble... that it somehow makes you noble and admirable – I urge you to consider that it may be holding you back from having the impact you were created to have in this world. The world needs what you have to offer it.

Which brings us full circle back to the second part of the brilliant quote by Marianne Williamson:

"Who am I to be brilliant, gorgeous, talented, fabulous? Actually, who are you not to be? You are a child of God. You playing small doesn't serve the world."

Our personal brand is more than our expertise; it's a harmonious blend of who we are, what we stand for, and how we communicate that to the world. Our confidence in that is our secret weapon – the driving force behind a resonating personal brand that captivates, influences, and leaves a lasting impact.

Self-confidence grows quickly as we align our core essence with our messages. It's a journey from self-doubt to self-assuredness, supported by the pillars of uniqueness, congruency, and elegance; having a deep-rooted belief in ourselves and a profound understanding of our significance and the value we bring.

Confidence as a personal brand requires a similar trust in our ability to communicate, connect, and make an impact.

This inner confidence reflects in everything we say and do as a brand.

In sharing our message, focus shifts from external responses to inner alignment. **This paradigm shift, from measuring validation to knowing we are valuable, energises our content creation.** The mind gremlins may persist, because we are still human, but they lose their grip as authenticity and purpose guide our expression.

Reflection Questions:

1. How can I cultivate a deeper belief in my own abilities and uniqueness?

2. What holds me back from stepping into bigger opportunities or taking risks?

3. How can I shift my focus from external validation to internal alignment?

4. In what ways can I infuse authenticity into my brand expression?

5. How does aligning my core essence with my messages impact the way I connect with my audience?

6. What transformations have I observed in my personal brand when I exude genuine self-confidence?

Chapter 10

Expanding Your Influence

Being influential isn't something you "do",
it's something you "are".

When you are a personal brand, influence is the biproduct of fully embracing and expressing your true identity in a way that connects. We become influential just by "being" – and the degree is determined by the level people connect to us, and the extent we allow our authentic selves to be expressed.

Just like the sun radiates warmth and light because of what it is – and we see and feel that when we observe it directly, we also feel it even if its presence is only visible through clouds or reflection on the moon.

Influence is *"the power to change or affect someone or something—especially the power to cause changes without directly forcing those changes to happen."*

I had a massive wake-up call recently when on the same day, I heard from TWO people in my network, completely separate of each other, that they often feel like giving up with their business, but they don't because they watch me and know my story and think, "If Nina can do it, I can too".

Influence is the end goal for why anyone would want to build a personal brand. What influence you want to have will vary for each individual, but ultimately, it's getting your brand to a place where it will motivate your audience to make a decision or inspire them to take an action.

At the start of this book (Chapter 1), we looked at the resistance people have to pressure tactics, fear, negativity or manipulation, and while the principles of influence are neutral in and of themselves, the way they've been used in the past has left a bitter taste in many mouths. The opposite is also true. When influence is motivated by a desire to make a positive difference, we can lift people up and have this impact just by having people in our presence, in our world – virtual or actual. The way the impact and influence plays out can unfold in the most synchronous and surprising of ways.

Authentic Growth: Beyond Perfection

One of the most memorable scenes of 2013 was when actress Jennifer Lawrence tripped while walking up to the stage to collect an Oscar in 2013. An infamous moment, which Vogue

Magazine called more of a "splat" than a fall. The same magazine however, credited this moment, and her handling of it, with changing the nature and influence of celebrity forever.

Clearly feeling the embarrassment, Jennifer didn't hide away and pretend the moment didn't happen. Instead, she adeptly made light of the incident, injected humour and acknowledging that it is what it is – in her words "really embarrassing".

What happened next was the catalyst for a whole new era of celebrity life – instead of tabloid shaming, she became the hero for her relatability and authenticity. Fans rallied around her and other celebrities took notes – and quite quickly cottoned on to the appeal of imperfection – and that it didn't negatively impact on the commercial aspect of what they did – if anything, it enhanced it.

It became a defining moment as personal brands became more open about sharing the parts of them that the average person could relate to and releasing the need for perfection and professionalism at every turn.

A study named the *Beautiful Mess Effect (American Psychological Association 2018)* showed that people imagining themselves in those situations felt weak and inadequate. On the other hand, if they imagined someone else in the same exact same situation that would make them feel inadequate, they perceived that person as desirable and good. Related to the *Beautiful Mess Effect,* the *Pratfall Effect* is the social phenomenon in which the favourability of a mistake is directly proportional to the individual's perceived competence. That is to say, the more competent you are, the more a mistake endears you to the people who witness it.

We looked in Chapter 2 about how the connection we have is directly linked to how we make someone feel, it's similar with influence. Except influence isn't "crafted" in the same way as content can be. It just is. It's more "cause and effect". Influence is an automatically generated biproduct of who we are and how we show up.

When it comes to our brand, content and message, the invitation (and the challenge) is go deep, find the gold, reflect on the past, ponder the future – but be open to sharing the shitty experiences too. It's natural to feel self-conscious about vulnerably sharing your experiences when you're in the thick of it, but it may surprise you to know that how you are perceived by others may actually be very different as a result.

When Mess Interrupts Magnificence

I was out on an early Sunday walk, in deep reflection by the water behind my house, walking the circuit that spans a few footbridges and loops around the river. Whenever I do this I stop at the park bench in the little park-like section of the riverbank opposite my house to admire the view and feel deep gratitude for where my life has brought me, despite the turbulent ups and downs.

On this glorious autumn morning I was struck by the clarity in the water and stopped to take a picture to remind me of this moment. Looking at the picture I'd just taken, the reflection in the water was so clear, it drew me into a deep train of thought, reflecting on many things (life, experiences, dreams etc.) So many lessons and ideas were coming to me in that moment. I was thinking "wow this is powerful, I should probably share this" – and my head went to formulating which angle I would take around that.

While deep in thought, all of a sudden, I felt something slimy on my hand. Warm and fresh from the bird flying overhead. It immediately took my focus out my very deep reflective space to the "here and now". Thankfully, said bird's deposit landed on my hand, not my head, but the timing and irony of it was not lost on me.

My focus immediately went from my dreams, and onto my slimy dirty hand. I had one thing on my mind in that moment. – Clean the hand but don't let it detract from this deep moment of focus. Gah!

But then I got to thinking – isn't this exactly like life? We're in this beautiful place and then out of the blue, some random sh*t drops into our life.

Our first instinct of course is to deal with it. And we absolutely need to do that. But once it's dealt with, how about being open to how that becomes part of our story? Framed in a way that's insightful & helpful to others?

The more I thought about THAT I realised wow, that was the message for me to share to my community that day. I could have made the piece about my ponderings and reflections and that would have been "nice".

But sharing about how I got shat on by a bird in my beautiful, reflective moment that makes the share so much more interesting (and human), right?! So, I guess that's the point. When it comes to how you share your message, go deep, find the gold, reflect on the past, ponder the dream – but be open to sharing the sh*!ty experiences too. (Once you've dealt with them – and in a way that shares a learning or principle. Not as a way of processing – we have journals and therapists for that!)

The human experience is a paradox of magnificent and messy.

Interestingly (or perhaps frustratingly), these are often unfolding at the same time. Many of us are creating content about what it is we "do" – but as we have seen, it's so much more powerful if we can inject the essence of who we "are", too. Because we are all human and people relate to those moments so much more than the picture-perfect ones.

The Science of Influence

The scientifically validated principles that drive influence have been explored in Cialdini's literary classic *Influence: The Psychology of Persuasion*, and many of the shifts in the psychology of marketing, sales and branding can be attributed to these principles.

Just like a knife, which has the power to heal in the hands of a surgeon, or hurt, in the hands of a robber, the principles are neutral in themselves. There have been many examples demonstrating the capacity of the principles used ethically to effect powerful social change. But negative manipulations have also been the catalyst for the increasing resistance to many of the mainstream marketing methods over the last few decades.

When you are a personal brand, it is worth being aware of the principles, so you can evaluate your own approach to building influence in your sphere.

These principles are:

Reciprocity:

People tend to give back to others who have given to them. This taps into our strong collective sense of social obligation. The key with reciprocity is to be first to give, and to do so in a way that is personalised, meaningful and unexpected.

Scarcity:

People inherently want more of the thing they can have less of. It's important to note the item also needs to have perceived value in order to be scarce – but when both these factors are in place desire increases without changing any of the other variables.

Authority:

People follow the lead of credible, knowledgeable experts. There is security that the information or direction they receive is solid, however for trust to be formed the authority needs to communicated through a third party, or be "shown not told" by the subject.

Consistency:

People will make decisions aligned with things they've said or done in the past – where the initial commitment has been voluntary, active and public. It plays to our desire to short-cut decision making and also to our sense of integrity as we follow through decisions we've made previously, even if they are micro-commitments.

Liking:

People are more easily influenced by people they like – there are chemical factors at play here. Smiles, receiving genuine compliments and alignment to mutual goals and values build rapport, and tap into human need for aspiration, sympathy or desire.

Social Proof:

People look to the actions and behaviours of others, who are similar to themselves, to drive their own actions. Tapping into the human desire to experience pleasure or avoid pain, the rational mind sees this as a way to "de-risk" and reduce negative consequences, or short-cut effort to pleasure. So, if people are considering engaging with your brand, they'll want to hear from people like them who have already done so.

Unity:

Unity is the bond formed by a shared identity two people experience – whether perceived or actual. There is a sense of validation, empathy and "feeling seen" which taps into the human desire for significance, and deep "connection" which comes from feeling "at one" with a person, brand or value.

What happened with Jennifer Lawrence in 2013 and the ripple effect of it was also a classic outworking of "Unity" the 7th principle of influence as outlined by author Robert Cialdini. People form a bond with people who those regard as sharing their values and identity (or desired identity). As Jennifer embraced her imperfection, with grace, humility and full humanity, she inadvertently became a paragon of influence for celebrities everywhere, who began sharing their versions of their own imperfection.

With all of the above principles, sometimes they are consciously deployed, other times they exist in the background. Either way, they are active, and the challenge now is how to adapt them to how society, the human psyche, and the marketplace generally is evolving.

Influence Can Happen in Surprising Ways

I don't go out of my way to influence people, but I know it's a biproduct of me showing up and being me and helping people as I go along in my professional life.

A surprising example of influence transpired in a way beyond what I could have ever expected. In 2022, I experienced possibly the sweetest night of my then-25+-year marketing career. Being awarded *Life Member* of the *Australian Marketing Institute* is the most prestigious honour that the AMI awards: for outstanding service, achievement, and leadership in the marketing industry.

Of course, the ability to do marketing and leadership well, so as to receive recognition like this is a pretty big superpower in this day and age. The "shy me" riddled with self-doubt just a few years ago would have played that down. Me, on the other side of this inner work, can confidently and proudly own it.

But that's not where the influence happened, or why this was so special for me. I'd won other awards previously but the impact of this one was due to something way more significant. The explosion of joy I felt was due to what I believe it signals for others building a personal brand.

This chapter of my life started a few years ago, as I decided to completely walk away from the marketing agency I'd built and run for 20 years, because I wasn't enjoying the experience anymore, and I felt that something significant was missing. I also believed that the traditional agency model that we've had over the last few decades was heading towards its "use by" date.

It was interesting timing, because, as I explained earlier, I began that transition in 2018, the year that the agency won *"Best Marketing Agency"* at the same Marketing Excellence awards – a very weird time to decide to walk away. Nevertheless, I decided to opt-out of a system that wasn't serving me, personally, at the time.

With that choice came a big realisation; I could no longer hide behind the agency brand, the logo, and the polished and professional veneer that it represented. That was confronting at first, I felt a lot more exposed and vulnerable. Looking back, I was caught up in how my industry colleagues and peers would regard me – would I measure up, with no company name, just being "me"?

I found myself often second guessing the way I wrote, showed up on social media, at events, in meetings, how I presented, how professional I was, how personal I got. And of course, I was always feeling the need to demonstrate my technical expertise. That was just so exhausting. But because I truly love what I do professionally, my personal mission became to create a new way.

This was not an easy path as a hands-on parent of five young children, but one I was committed to. That meant removing those expectations about what I thought people wanted to see and making things easier by just being "fully me" everywhere I interacted and showed up. If those choices were going to affect how I was perceived in my industry, then so be it.

Turns out, in the last few years it no longer mattered to me whether I received recognition or how I was regarded by my peers and industry heroes. The impact being created was reward enough. I went all in on my *Marketing Me*® praxis, spoke, trained, mentored, wrote the book (here we are!), and regularly speak on this topic because it's something I so deeply believe in.

The fact is that marketing your brand is no longer just about getting your message and products in front of more people. Especially when you are a personal brand. It is about connecting with your audience in a deeper, more emotional way and to do that it's necessary to make people feel something with your marketing. My standout talent is in helping business leaders and experts do exactly this – as well as unlock and master the future of marketing as it's just unfolding. And I wanted to do more of it.

At my core I believed it was time to do marketing in a more human way, that feels good to you and to your audience so you can feel confident, clear, and energised in your marketing. Throwing the expectations out the window, I went all in on something I believed in and when I was no longer seeking it, along came the recognition.

That such a prestigious accolade happened was something I'm deeply grateful for, but the thing that overwhelmed me with joy was that it came on my own terms. What I equally love is what it signals to others: that we don't have to follow a linear path. Nor do we need to achieve perfection. We don't have to dull down our uniqueness to fit in just because that's the way people before us did it, or the way others are doing it now.

At the core of personal branding, influence is the goal. It varies for each individual, but the power to motivate decisions and inspire actions is the ultimate aim.

The realisation that influence is born from genuine connection, rather than pressure tactics or manipulation, sets the stage for a positive shift in the way we approach building our brands. Along with the commercial and professional benefits we experience because of our brand, it is extremely fulfilling to uplift and impact lives just by being ourselves.

The lesson is clear: **influence arises from authenticity, connection, and shared values.** Through this, as personal brands, we have the opportunity to shape perceptions and drive positive change in ourselves, our communities, and the world.

There's room for you to create your own path, and express your personality, without having to wonder if you are too much, even as a professional. With the right strategic approach, it's your most powerful asset. The world is changing, society is changing, and how we market ourselves is changing as well.

As we embrace our uniqueness, show up authentically, wrap our message in elegance, build our belief in ourselves – singularly and together our influence is making a difference. And not just in our places of business and work – but in our families, our homes, our communities, and beyond that, our world.

Reflection Questions:

1. How do I define influence in the context of my personal brand?

2. How can I authentically express my true identity to expand my influence?

3. Can I recall moments when my authenticity has positively influenced others?

4. How do I perceive the balance between authenticity and professional presentation?

5. Have I experienced a situation where my imperfections enhanced my influence?

6. Which of the influence principles resonate most with my personal brand values?

7. How can I incorporate the principles of influence into my personal branding strategy?

8. In what ways can I harness my influence to drive positive change in my field?

PART III

BUILDING A PERSONAL BRAND THAT CONNECTS

So now that you know a bit more about yourself and you're learning to design an improved way of relating to the world and your mission, this section takes everything you just discovered and teaches you how to start using it.

In an earlier chapter we looked at the personal brand exploration journey and how you can essentially split it into two parts: the *"inner" preparation* and the *"outer" permeation.*

In a time where we are completely overloaded with choices and marketing options it is helpful to have sound principles to follow. This framework for creating your brand is something you can come back to over and over to refine your focus and determine your next steps:

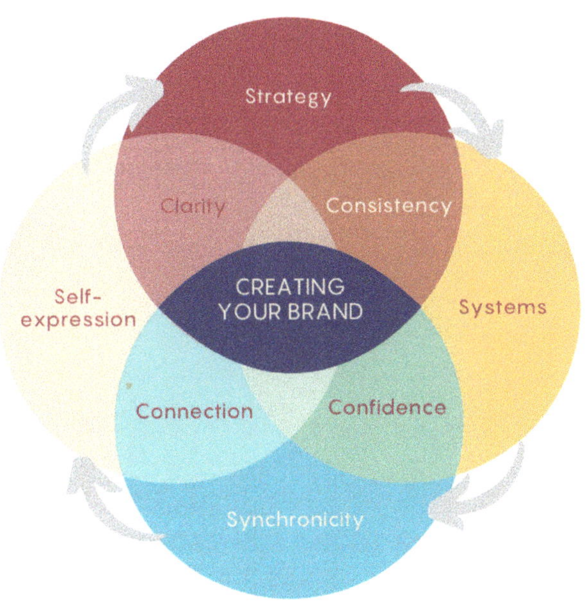

Each element in this diagram is a vital key to creating a magnetic, connected personal brand. But it's the inter-dependence of the elements that is where the power lies – it's definitely a case of the whole being far greater than the sum of the parts.

You'll be naturally stronger in one area than in others and that's ok. This section will show you how you can develop the other areas. Growth is a part of the journey and even the most experienced of people are inspired by watching others grow. People love the evolution. In fact, that's often way more interesting than someone emerging on the scene polished and professional with everything all together. If you're feeling resistance, know that it's perfectly normal, just view it as inviting your audience along with you and wherever you are at now is the right place for you to start. As you get comfortable sharing your own transformational journey, and integrating all of these elements, you'll find that will bond you to people in a far more powerful way, with far less effort.

CHAPTER 11

Self-Expression as a Superpower

We looked extensively at Self-Expression in Part II of this book – and unpacked the process to allowing your identity to emerge and be expressed.

While genuine self-expression is at the cornerstone of a personal brand it's important to see this in context with the other factors too. Pure expression that does not have commercial intent behind it is art. In the context we are looking at we are consciously allowing people to see parts of ourselves for the purpose of creating some sort of impact – in the world or in our business or professional life. It may be to attract customers, get a promotion or attract speaking invitations. Your purpose may not be monetary, it may be to inspire people to rally around a cause, help them shift a perspective, or take a course of action to improve their lives. The common denominator is that there is a clear bigger purpose that plays a key role in why and how we are sharing parts of ourselves with the world.

One of the biggest paradoxes is that there is now a marketplace obsession with:

1. The need to get a **commercial return** on your efforts. *(ok to be fair, this has always existed!)*
2. The driving need for **authenticity.**

Authenticity means a lot of different things to different people. There are two important aspects of authenticity: the first is that you need to be recognisable and unique, the second is that you need to be genuine. This isn't a surprise in the context of the definition of the word, or if you are thinking about handbags for example. It's easy to understand that for a designer item to be considered authentic it needs to be **recognisable, unique and genuine**. But when you think of it in the context of marketing it becomes food for thought. From this, one can easily draw the link between authenticity and the need for self-expression for it to be effective.

The bottom line is, for maximum impact we need to be self-expressed and strategic, such that both become your default way of thinking, acting, and being. It IS possible and it IS liberating.

Linking self-expression with other aspects of our marketing is both an art and a science. One of the favourite parts of my work is when I get to help visionaries, multi-talented professionals, and business owners get clarity on how to show up in a way that's both gloriously self-expressed (in a way that lights them up!) yet ingeniously strategic. Because it's all sitting in there, ready to get unleashed, and when it does... get ready to pop.

> ## Reflection Question:
>
> What's unique about you that you could be recognised for that's aligned to your commercial intent?

CHAPTER 12

Strategy that Strengthens

When it comes to marketing, the current reality is 3–5 year strategies don't hold the same place they used to. Right now, people struggle to get their heads around planning for the next 6 months, let alone a year in advance, because goal posts and game rules are changing all the time. Even in marketing, the decades-long "normal way of doing things" is evolving so quickly, so the way we need to approach strategy is different.

It's time to simplify everything; including strategy.

Below are five important questions that will help you simplify and strengthen your strategy. These will act as guard-rails to ensure your actions are focused on the right outcomes. I recommend you keep these in mind whenever you are making any marketing decisions around your personal brand or business, determining your messaging and positioning, and creating and distributing content in order to ensure that any actions you are taking are aligned to both your current and future goals.

What do you want to be known for?

This might be different to 3 years ago and may well be different in another 3 years. When you're a personal brand, this is completely ok and to be embraced.

Be easy to understand, clear and concise in everything you share, and get your messaging dialled in.

Rather than just focusing purely on the intellectual "knowing" about who you are and what you do, there is much power in harnessing the emotional "knowing". "How do you want your audience to FEEL about you?" is another great question to ask when you are approaching this.

How are you commercialising your brand?

What is your plan to monetise your personal brand? Is it to build your business, further your career, get a promotion, find new customers, attract business partners/sponsorships? In the case of a charity or social cause, you may not be profiting financially, but you are out to inspire action and change. And that takes finance, whatever source it comes from, to sustain it.

It's important to think about the bigger reason for why you are building your brand, and being clear on who you need to be in front of, what action you want them to take and how you'll know if you're successful.

Be easy to buy. Don't do all the hard yards of getting attention and profile without a smooth way to turn that into revenue or measurable impact.

What is your main marketing objective?

You can't be focusing on everything, all the time, so think about what is the highest priority objective? Is it customer awareness, nurturing, conversion? Or getting in front of the right stakeholders? Opening doors to high profile collaborations? And of course, it's imperative to understand and be clear on who your customers are.

In a traditional marketing strategy, especially with a "logo" or corporate brand, market research would typically have a much stronger focus. However, given our context here, personal brand research is definitely important and worth a mention, but it also needs to be balanced out in context of the other questions, too.

Be easy to connect with. And be clear about why you're doing the marketing actions you are taking.

What resources can you draw on?

Your marketing approach will be in a large part determined by the resources you have access to – which will include finance, experience, expertise, team, contractors, network, colleagues, peers, as well as your time, energy and health.

Consider what you have at your disposal and, without being over-ambitious, consider all your resources. Building a personal brand can be approached in so many ways. Rarely is it a case of paid advertising. In most cases it's a combination of personal action, and strategic collaborations.

Be easy to work with. When you are the brand, your ability to have people share your content, introduce, collaborate with and support you will depend on how they feel about working with you.

What comes easily and is most enjoyable?

When you are the brand it's so important to protect yourself as the most important asset. Not pushing yourself too hard or placing unrealistic expectations on yourself is imperative. It makes it so much easier to stay on track if you do something that is light, easy and fun. As this means you are way more likely to actually DO it, than just intend to do it.

Be easy on yourself. It's also important to consider what resources YOU desire to bring into the marketing equation – and this will depend on the time you have, and desire to create and implement. As well as leaning towards your preferences and what you enjoy and feel most comfortable with – not doing things just because you think you "should" be doing them or because other people are doing them.

Remember you are unique – your way is the right way. Keep this in mind and you'll have more impact over the long term and enjoy better health along the way.

Strategy that Strengthens Takes the Pressure Off!

The good thing about a strategy is it's generally not reliant on one single action or event – rather a well thought through plan that is executed bit by bit over a period of time – adapted and tweaked as necessary.

A great way to understand strategy in the context of a personal brand is to imagine building a house.

The strategy is like the design and plan that you're working with. Obviously, it can be changed and re-drawn as you go along, but you've got a clear plan for what you're building. It means you're not placing undue emphasis on a particular brick or window or beam, as you understand everything works together over the long term, to build what you desire to create.

It also helps you understand where to put different things. Consider the questions asked above as strong foundations, which you need to have in place before you start building. They will give you a general idea of the size, aesthetic and end goal for why you are building it.

This approach helps you understand that all the individual pieces – bricks, timber, nails, windows, doors - all fulfil a purpose when working together. Translating this to marketing, this helps you not place undue emphasis on any one particular activity (e.g. social media posts, or an event, or campaign) because you see them as what they are: small elements that all work together to create the desired outcome over the long term.

To be able to sustain small elements working together over the long term, it's imperative that we make it "easy". This is why we short-cut our work and our load, when we are easy to understand, easy to buy, easy to connect with, easy to work with, and easy on ourselves.

Key Strategy Mindset Shifts

Here are four things that will help you develop a 'strategy that strengthens'.

Each of these will help you become **easy to understand, easy to buy, easy to understand, easy to connect with and work with, and easy on yourself.**

- **Do less, but be focused and intentional**
  It might feel like you're moving slower than you'd like to in the short-term, but because of that you will be more able to sustain your efforts over the long term, which is what really counts.

- **No more random acts of content**
  Knee-jerk or ad-hoc content won't help you get known for something and build a strong digital footprint. Putting out something "for the sake of it" might be tempting but if it means you confuse your audience it's hardly worth the hard-earned sweat and effort.

- **Keep your desired outcome front & centre**
  When you have a clear picture of the end goal and why you are building your brand, you can work out what steps you need to take, and what could be the key milestones and markers along the way that will keep you on track.

- **Adjust your marketing objectives for each season**
  As a personal brand your ability to invest into growing it is going to ebb and flow in the different seasons of your life. You're a human not a machine, and it's important to remember that what this quarter looks like might be different from last quarter or next quarter. I like to work in 90-day "seasons" and take a "seasonal" approach to commitments, priorities and where I will put my efforts. This is based on what I have on, my family situation, my business, and how I am feeling about things generally.

There are so many variables in building a personal brand and no "one size fits all" approach that will work in every situation. You will increase your impact and success as a brand as you leverage the timeless principles of marketing (particularly strategy, creativity, and analytical thinking) and adapt them to your personal situation in a way that is do-able and flexible and ultimately supports the long-term growth of your brand.

We aren't all professional marketing strategists, but we all have a personal brand. So the most important thing to remember is that we have a message that matters, a unique perspective and voice for the world, and a role to play in creating impact in our own significant way.

Having a simple strategy in place to direct our efforts ensures we're focusing our efforts in the right place, and aligning our actions with our long-term plan and goals.

CHAPTER 13

Systems for Sustainability

Whether it's business, branding, home life, or health I'm constantly on the lookout for how I can create or improve systems that enable me to do what I do with greater ease, and even fun and joy. James Clear, in his book *Atomic Habits* states, *"You don't rise to the level of your goals, you fall to the level of your systems."*[10]

Having the right systems helps keep us on track and prevent burnout. Before I had solid systems in place, I constantly felt exhausted and like I had no real rhythm around how I was building my personal brand. Once I figured out the right systems for creating high calibre content consistently and supporting it with solid branding and processes that power it at the backend, everything totally changed.

When it comes to what made the difference and knowing which systems will serve you best here are my top takeaways:

- **Know your end goals**
  Before you spend time setting up systems, make sure they align with your bottom line.
- **Start small and layer**
  Only add something new once you've had something working consistently for a month, and build from there.
- **Document every single step**
  Take the guesswork and randomness out of what you're doing and don't delegate anything that doesn't have a clear process in place.

If you're just getting started, or have a fabulous strategy but it's gone to custard, your best next step is to start with a very simple plan. Make this plan ten times simpler than you think you want to, don't try and do too much too soon. Consistency over the long term is way better than sporadic efforts.

If your marketing to-do list feels overwhelming, don't fret, it can be so much easier. The key is chunking it down into bite-size tasks and doing them regularly – at the same time each week is ideal. Small steps done consistently trump massive flurries of activity sporadically because building a brand is a cumulative process over a long period of time, not a once-and-done affair. I'm firm in the belief that an hour spent wisely once a week for three months will yield greater results than a full week of concerted effort done once in that time.

Contrary to what many people think, systems do not need to be complex, nor take a lot of energy, and you don't need a big team. You don't even need any team if you're just starting out! It's about creating a system that is right for YOU. Systems are not "one size fits all" or even "one size fits most"! But what a simple and appropriate system *will* do is give you freedom. This allows you to spend way less energy thinking about and doing marketing, and more time to do the things that are most enjoyable and energising for you!

Do Your Marketing in an Hour a Week

As a personal brand, here's some sobering, real-world, marketing advice you won't hear very often (if at all!).

If you're spending more than an hour of YOUR time on marketing each week, you're overdoing it, and doing more than you need to.

Too many people yo-yo between doing "too much" and "nothing". In those times where they go full throttle, it just takes too much energy for it to be sustainable, and ends up eating into personal, social or self-care time.

But on the other hand, there are a whole lot of aspiring brands not doing anything because they don't know where to start or put their focus.

Too many people are out there looking for the "magic beans" that fairy-tale Jack stumbled upon when trading his cow. They're intent on pursuing the elusive "beanstalk strategy". Thinking it'll shoot their business into exponential growth overnight. Unfortunately, it doesn't exist.

With nearly 3 decades of doing this, working with over 1000 brands, I've witnessed a lot of different growth journeys. And sure, in the personal brand space I've seen people shoot up seemingly overnight. Where chance, opportunity and an extraordinary amount of sweat equity and hustle combined. But it's rarely, if ever sustainable. Especially when you are a personal brand. That has a life. That does other stuff besides marketing. And without a huge team.

It doesn't happen consuming countless YouTube videos, blogs, late-night googling, watching more webinars and events, and filling your head with endless online chats and discussions. Definitely not how I want to live, work and be. I've also done "all the things" over the years, through fad after fad, era after "new era", in an effort to understand and figure out what works. I use this understanding to create easier ways for myself and my clients.

It starts – and continues – with small, focused, decisive actions. When you're a personal brand, you should aim to have a foundational system you can sustain in an hour a week.

Anything more – it's likely not sustainable for more than a month or two. You'll dip out and it'll end up in the "too hard basket". You'll lose interest, momentum and become the yo-yo. And we all know that does. Not. Feel. Good. On the other hand, anything less than an hour a week, and you're missing a massive opportunity to tap into one or two highly leveraged actions, that are UNIQUE to you, to:

- *build your audience,*
- *be in front of them regularly,*
- *build the connection that leads to sales and bigger impact.*

Having a one-hour-a-week marketing commitment is only possible if you have a smooth system, so that the time you're putting in is leveraged.

There's no "one system" or platform or approach that's right for everyone.

But there are three basic "types of systems" that work together to create connection and impact with ease:

Content Systems for Success

A content CREATION system gives you agency.

As a personal brand **the source content needs to be YOU.** It's not something you can delegate or outsource. This is giving away agency over your voice, and your message.

Sure, you can enlist support to help you polish your ideas, edit, format or turn your raw ideas in to something people can consume, but the thoughts and ideas need to originate with you if you're serious about building your brand and connecting with people.

If you wait until you're inspired, motivated, in the right place, at the right time, and all the stars need to be aligned for you to create there will always be a reason why it doesn't happen. Putting in place a habitual system where you express a thought for the purpose of content, once a week will ensure you have a steady stream of fresh content at the ready with minimal effort.

A content REPURPOSING system gives you agility.

This is one area where outside help is not only okay, it's recommended! Whether that is human or technology! Turning your original ideas, creativity into different formats and mediums makes total sense – and is where leverage and multiplication will kick in.

There are several technologies I use and recommend for my own repurposing and that of my clients, I share them at this link www.ninachristian.com/tools.

A content DISTRIBUTION system gives you amplification.

This is possibly the most important of all the systems, yet the one most people overlook. They post their hard-earned content on social media and hope for the best, not realising that there are so many other ways that content can get in front of more eyeballs.

Again, if you have to perform mental gymnastics each time you want to publish and distribute a piece of content, your reach will be far more limited. However, if you have a system in place to distribute your content in multiple places, the system will do most of the heavy lifting!

Your distribution system needs to be set up in a way that keeps you:

Visible

You actively PUSH out your content to where people may come across your brand in the course of their everyday activities. (social, email, events).

The upside of this, is that you can actively control how many people your brand is exposed to based on your effort and it keeps you front of mind. The downside is that it generally requires ongoing effort and if that stops, the visibility slows down too.

Findable

Being in the places where people are likely to look when they are looking for solutions around what it is you do (search, YouTube, Pinterest, Directories etc.) so you can PULL them in.

The advantage here is that time starts to work for you not against you, and like compound interest, your digital footprint increases cumulatively over time, as you continue to make small deposits on a regular basis.

Shareable

This is the highest leveraged option out of all – it's where you have other people putting your content and brand in front of their audiences. And the authority factor is amplified by the PRAISE of your brand that's inherent by the share.

The numbers may be small or large, but quantity is less relevant. What counts is the trust and credibility factor – especially when your content is shared by key people of influence in your industry.

However, the implementation is finely nuanced to reflect you and to work for you.

And that's when it becomes something of a *"choose your own adventure"* where you may benefit from the guidance and support of a specialist to help you identify distribution opportunities that you can't see yourself. They can guide you to get you set up correctly, so you don't end up down rabbit holes investing time, money and energy into things that don't serve your business vision and strategy, or personal preferences.

The worst thing you can do is try to do what's working for someone else, but doesn't gel for you.

It's critical to your success to **find the thing that lights you up – and build a system around that** – so that marketing becomes such a fun, energising and impactful activity – that not just builds your brand but drives (and draws in!) sales as well.

The path to effective marketing for a personal brand is paved with the right systems. **Systems are the backbone that keeps you on track and safeguards against burnout.** Marketing, especially as a personal brand, shouldn't drain you. You shouldn't be oscillating between overexertion and inaction.

The journey from exhaustion and aimlessness to empowerment and joy begins when you harness the magic of systems. I've seen first-hand that the path to success isn't through "magic beans" or unrealistic overnight transformations. it's through small, focused, and decisive actions. As a personal brand, your marketing shouldn't require endless hours or a large team.

Remember, there's no one-size-fits-all approach. Your system should reflect you and your brand, as something that energises and resonates with you. When marketing feels good to both you and your audience, it becomes a powerful tool for impact and sharing your message with the world.

CHAPTER 14

Synchronicity Over Striving

Last year, I had to take one of my children to the eye hospital. It was a serious situation where I was told urgent treatment was required, and so all the other competing family priorities were temporarily paused while the eye was attended to. Those priorities included the plans of one of my other children, who had a birthday party scheduled that same morning.

Once the eye had been saved, I returned home from the hospital feeling utterly exhausted. I was trying to think about the myriad things I needed to do next, among which was console a distressed child, because they couldn't attend the birthday party as planned.

I had been at the hospital since the early hours of the morning, for the second time that week. So, when another child unleashed their frustration on me I had a very human reaction, and realised I was not going to be able to hold it together much longer. I did what I often do in those situations when I'm overcome with emotion – I put myself in a time-out. We have a park around the corner, so I took some space to sit on the grass, process all of what was going on and calm down.

After I had calmed myself down, I returned home ready to resume the day's program, which included driving my daughter to a friend's place.

There was just one problem.

I couldn't find my keys.

Usually, I hang my keys on the hook by the door. On that particular day, because I was in a complete daze, I had no idea what I had done with them. We looked high and low at home, and at the park, to no avail.

As I walked in the door from the park, one of my other kids told me the courier had just dropped off a package. The delivery was a beautiful, personalised, navy keyring from my friend and client, Oksana. I was floored. Oksana specialises in branded merchandise and is also my go-to for sourcing thoughtful gifts to use in my own marketing. Out of the blue, Oksana sent me this gift, which happened to arrive at precisely the right time, just 15 minutes after I'd lost my keys. I felt that there was a comforting inter-connectedness about what was unfolding

The next day I went back to the park for another look for my keys. The long grass had been mown, so it was now easier to see. Some sparkling metal caught my eye and amongst the lawn clippings, I saw my keys, a mangled mess, in the grass. The gold leather keyring that was on the keyring had been completely obliterated. It turns out I had inadvertently taken my keys with me the day before and left them on the grass, where I had been sitting and crying. Several of the keys had been destroyed due to the mowing, but thankfully the important ones (house, car, mailbox) were intact. I went home and put them on the beautiful new keyring that Oksana had sent me, with joy and excitement.

Oksana had no way of knowing my gold leather keyring (which had my initials on it) was going to be destroyed a few days later. Yet, she sent me a beautiful leather keyring with my initials on it because she felt inspired to do so. She's always in service to her clients, and because she does her marketing with such heart and intention, the care and connection is something that can be tangibly felt by the recipient.

On this occasion, it was more than just a thoughtful gift – it turned out to be an expression of synchronicity that cohesively served her business, my life, her brand, and my content. I felt more deeply connected to her as a supplier and industry colleague. And now each time I look at or hold the keyring I'm reminded of that encounter.

Have you ever noticed connections that just "happen" in a way you would never plan or expect, that feel like a freaky co-incidence, or even fate? This is the magic of synchronicity. Synchronicity is a concept first introduced by analytical psychologist Carl G. Jung *"to describe circumstances that appear meaningfully related yet lack a causal connection"*. Synchronicity is one of the most powerful forces in marketing. It can't be manufactured, but it can be encouraged.

A Completely New Way of (Not) Thinking!

Synchronicity is more than just about joining dots – dots being things that already exist, which our strategic brain can figure out how to link. A synchronous approach is about "allowing", even "inviting" new connections to come. The idea that seemingly unrelated things somehow have a relationship, even if it's not immediately obvious. If you can entertain the idea that everything is connected, then it's not a stretch to believe that anything can be connected. There is an idea of infinite possibility around creating connection between any two or more things. This is the new and future way of doing content.

There are three powerful elements at play in the synchronous approach to content.

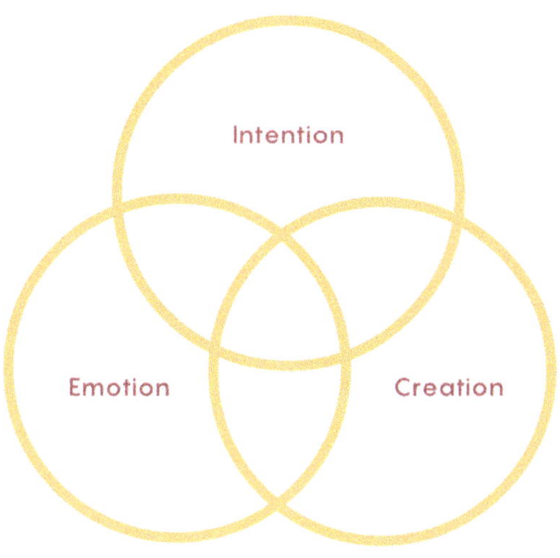

Intention

Our intention is the catalyst that allows these connections to be revealed. Our expertise, capability, and competency are still relevant but as we build the muscle of setting intentions, before we create content, we create space for synchronous events to unfold.

In the case of the keyring, there was also clear intention by Oksana to be of service to me as a client, and a desire for this to be a memorable experience for me.

When I recounted this incident in my own content, the intention I infused into it was for people to "get" the power of synchronicity and how things happen to us that we can use in our content, and also to demonstrate how "stunning stories" help us connect with our audiences.

Emotion

Emotion is the heart, the feelings, and the personal energy you infuse into what you're creating. It's the aspect of your content that makes your audience "feel" and the bridge to a deep and meaningful emotional connection.

With the keyring, there was emotion injected into that through care and thoughtfulness, right through to embossing my initials on the keyring. And beyond the initials, the emotion was transmitted via the timing of the delivery.

On my part, when I created content about the incident after the fact, I injected deep emotion into that content (e.g. email and blog) which was, in turn, felt by my audience.

Creation

Creation is the act of turning the connection possibilities into tangible realities. This is where we turn the synchronous events into synchronous content.

With the keys example, I turned that synchronous event into a social media post, an email and a blog – and now a story in my book. If you don't create something from it, it stays in your head, and you miss the opportunity to put it out into the world.

This worked at multiple levels to strengthen our connection, as well as her brand and my brand at the same time, through the timing and content that emerged from it.

When you have intention, emotion and creation coming together synchronously, you have a powerhouse brand experience.

While it's not typical to have synchronous events happen at

will, when you proactively harness each of these three elements – intention, emotion and creation – for the purpose of connecting with your audience, not only do you have marketing and content that makes people feel something, you also create room for the unexpected and synchronous events to occur. Moreover, you are able to leverage these for both your brand and for strengthening the relationship with the people that you serve.

Reflection Questions:

1. **What is my intention behind my content creation?**
   Am I infusing it with genuine emotion and intention that aligns with my brand's values?

2. **How can I harness heart energy in my content?**
   How can I incorporate emotions, empathy, and relatable experiences that resonate with my audience?

3. **Am I open to perceiving and creating connections that may not be immediately obvious?**
   Can I embrace the idea that everything is connected and create space for those connections to unfold naturally?

4. **Do I have a system in place to capture insights and act on them?**
   How can I set up a structure that enables me to turn synchronistic moments into impactful content?

5. **Am I willing to explore the infinite possibilities of creating connections between seemingly unrelated aspects of my life and business?**

6. **How can I cultivate a sense of curiosity and wonder in my content creation process?**
   Can I approach content creation with an open mind, ready to receive unexpected insights?

7. **How can I integrate heart energy into my interactions with my audience?**
   How can I make them feel seen, heard, and understood through my content?

The Heart Connection

In the past, we have been used to leading with our expertise, and appealing to the brain which is very logical. However logical isn't the same as being effective. People's cognitive capacity to receive and process information these days is way less than it used to be, whereas their **emotional receptors** are so much more open to receive and bypass the logical.

One way to rapidly increase the potency of your content is to harness heart energy and infuse more emotion into what you're creating. This way, it's *felt,* and not merely *thought about,* by your audience.

Physiologically, the heart is a powerful organ that generates an electromagnetic field, often referred to as the "heart's electromagnetic field" or "heart coherence." These energetic forces are measurable (typically by electrocardiography like an ECG or EKG machine or magnetometers). A study by scientists at the Heartmath Institute showed that heart energy (also known as cardioelectromagnetic communication) is the most powerful source of electromagnetic energy in the human body.

Heart energy can impact the body's physiological processes and overall well-being. The heart's electromagnetic field also interacts with the electromagnetic fields of other people and the environment, and while this is more difficult to quantify, studies suggest that people can synchronise their heart rhythms when in close proximity or engaged in positive social interactions.

Metaphorically speaking, heart energy refers to emotions,

feelings, and qualities that are often associated with the heart, such as love, compassion, empathy, and connection. Both metaphorically and literally, the energy of the heart has a measurable influence on the world surrounding it. This is what we are tapping into when we explore "heart energy" in the context of connecting with people as a personal brand.

If we look at how to harness heart energy to receive and make meaning of these "interconnected" ideas heart energy also paves the way for these synchronous connections to come *to* you and *through* you – which you can then infuse into your content.

Sometimes those connections are really obvious – and there's nothing wrong with that! But sometimes they'll be less obvious – some really cool connections will come from the ether. If you want your content to go next level, open yourself to the possibility that what happens in your business is connected to what happens in your life, which is connected to your brand, which is connected to your wellbeing. Just like my story with the keys.

As you start to be open to perceiving those connections, and as you start to unpack them and join the dots, you will inevitably give people the "OMG" experience, leaving them thinking, "I didn't see how those things were related, but they totally are!" And that lights people up too, because it sparks something inside of them.

Then you have something truly unique – and it's highly relevant, powerful, and potent. For many, this is a new approach to content – but it bypasses the strain and slog of trying to do it the old way. The more I live and do business out of this space the easier it gets, and the lighter it feels to build a powerful personal brand, because you bypass "volume of effort" and go straight to "high-potency moments."

It might seem counter-intuitive, but even the act of setting up a simple system can unlock a new way of approaching and doing: Strategic Synchronicity. This is the ability to create simpler and more aligned ways of creating content and things that demand less of you, and yet have so much more impact. Because when you have a system in place that makes it easier to take action on insights that come *from* you, you make it easier for yourself to be open to synchronicity and receive new connections as they come *to* you.

Infused into your content, this can multiply the connection factor of your content exponentially, as well as help you create with so much more ease.

Intention Is the Catalyst for Connection

The threads of synchronicity, heart energy, and content creation weave together to unveil a new paradigm for personal branding and content strategy. Synchronicity takes us beyond the realm of causality, allowing for connections that aren't immediately apparent but carry profound meaning. This is the essence of the new way of doing content—inviting connections to unfold rather than merely joining pre-existing dots.

In this approach, intention becomes the catalyst for these connections, and the infusion of heart energy magnifies their potency. Intention matters because authenticity is impossible to fake.

At its core, synchronicity is about welcoming and inviting new connections that might not be immediately apparent. The concept of synchronicity is an intriguing phenomenon where connections materialise in unexpected ways. We can be observant about how those happen, and the fascinating part is our ability to make these happen – by harnessing the power of intention, emotion and creation.

Our intentions set the stage for these connections, while infusing heart energy into our content amplifies their impact. By embracing the notion that everything is connected, we open ourselves to infinite possibilities, turning synchronous events into meaningful content.

Energetically, emotion trumps intellect. And that's why if there's no emotion in your marketing it won't have the energetic connection your audience is craving.

Every piece of content has the potential to be a bridge, connecting you to your audience through the power of the heart, and transfer energy. So, a final question for you: **if you were to metaphorically put your marketing on an ECG, would it show a healthy, strong, and regular heartbeat, or would it be flatlining?**

Over the last four chapters we explored the components of a holistic personal brand, and how they work together and support each other.

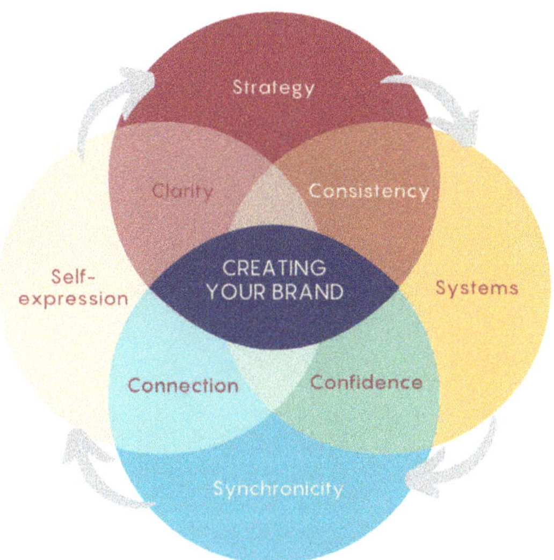

As this diagram indicates, when Self-Expression, Strategy, Systems and Synchronicity function in alignment, the natural result is a virtuous cycle, and the four big challenges of *Clarity, Confidence, Consistency* and *Connection* are inherently and "automagically" addressed and overcome, as the core brand elements continue to build upon another, taking you to new levels, personally and professionally.

You emerge as an individual with a profound awareness of your identity, strong confidence in your abilities, an influential presence in your expression, as you forge a compelling and impactful personal brand. Your efforts become precise, channelled to the right places at the right times, maximising your leverage and sustainability – which also lead to a better quality of life!

CHAPTER 15
The Power of Simple

In an overloaded world, where we are all info-fatigued, we need SIMPLE.

I know it can be overwhelming with all the advice and "shoulds" and "oughts" coming at us on the daily, I feel it too. But I also know the cumulative power of clear, decisive, and small but mighty actions.

When it comes to marketing, it might feel like we want to do a lot. However, we need to be realistic and I'm a big believer that **simple is always better than stopping** and feeling paralysed by the question of what to focus on. It's better than letting it slide because you just don't have the bandwidth to execute your elaborate plan, or those elusive and judgemental "shoulds".

When I was running a marketing agency with a team, doing content creation for corporate brands, our content creation systems and methodologies were complex with lots of moving parts and pieces and various messages in market to ensure variety. I used my drive for efficiency, which has been honed as a mum of lots of kids, to find the fastest and simplest and most effective way of doing something. I have applied this to the complex task of content creation for multiple modalities and channels.

Often these systems were very sophisticated. To the client it was beautifully simple. The CEO would spend an hour with us a month and from that we would produce 6 months' worth of unique and high-quality thought leadership content. However, it was a long process to design, test and optimise those systems at our backend.

Through experimentation, we got it to a place where there was a genuine ease over it. Then I realised the power of these systems and solutions could benefit more brands than the B2B larger businesses we were serving. Especially those I most wanted to help – powerful voices who are creating an impact in the world, but were stuck when it came to marketing.

So, I took those sophisticated methods of content creation, adapted them, and started spoon-feeding them to business owners and other marketers. It was a game-changer for small brands that had been struggling with content creation who had looked everywhere for a better way and not found one. Relief was at hand!

Then, something happened. Two years later, we entered a pandemic and people's ability to execute changed. What was an acceptable amount of focus on content, was too much now, and I noticed people not able to keep up anymore. The best of intentions didn't translate to the content library they wanted. I realised I needed to simplify, so simplify I did.

Each year after that I've also simplified, to the point where at the time of writing this, the systems are the simplest ever. I now recommend that if you are a personal brand, you need a repeatable system that you can do within an hour a week, or else it isn't sustainable – even with the best intentions.

And like compound interest, committing to a system and sticking with it is where the leverage power is. This is good news if you find complex systems un-executable, you're not alone, it's pretty much everyone these days.

I didn't stumble on this by accident. Personally, it came out of necessity – having a compelling desire to grow my brand and build my digital footprint, but limited in what I could do by the constraints of life. Then I realised, it wasn't just me. My clients, who were employees with jobs, entrepreneurs with clients to serve, leaders with teams, everyone has a legitimate reason why actually implementing the dream plan isn't doable – because we're human.

My obsession has been to simplify inputs, and leverage outputs. And being a parent to five children has given me the ability to fast-track simple ways to get things done.

Over the years, I've developed the ability to tap into this drive for efficiency as a way of identifying the highest leverage points. And by far, the most potent leverage point I've tapped into has been the efficiencies gained by eliminating unnecessary decisions.

Making Bigger, Better Decisions

The drive to optimise decision-making was birthed out of the things I'm most challenged with on a daily basis – **decision fatigue.**

It's astounding how many decisions we make daily. One piece of research puts the number around 35,000 decisions per day, for the average adult. *(Sollsich, 2016, published in the J Health Psychology Journal in 2022)*

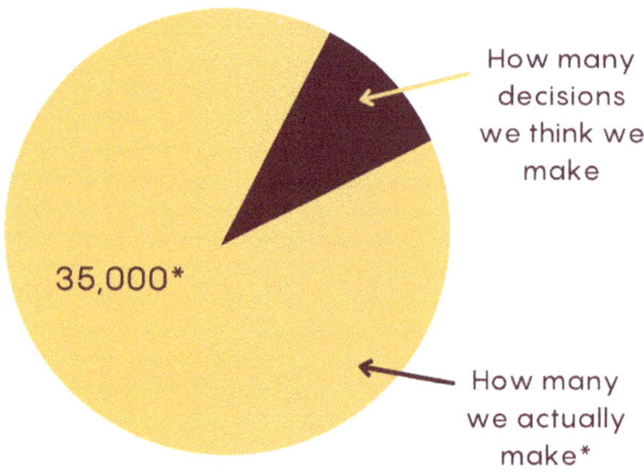

The number of decisions I need to make on any given day is mind-blowing, and as a result, I sometimes have instances when my brain involuntarily freezes and is incapable of making basic decisions like what to eat. My fridge could be full of food and yet the simple act of going to the kitchen, choosing some food and serving it up might be just too much.

On the other days, I can do eight loads of washing in a day, because the tactile experience of washing and hanging and drying doesn't require focused thought, but folding one basket of dry washing is "too much" because it requires 40 micro-decisions as to who each item belongs to and where it goes.

I can load the dishwasher quite easily as everything is going in one location – but I find unloading sends my brain into a frenzy – because again it requires thought about where to put things.

My brain has a way of shutting down to conserve my energy for bigger decisions *(and thankfully I have little people who can help with dishes!)*

I'm not alone. I'm comforted by the fact Barack Obama faced similar challenges.

He famously told *Vanity Fair* magazine... *"You'll see I wear only gray or blue suits. I'm trying to pare down decisions. I don't want to make decisions about what I'm eating or wearing. Because I have too many other decisions to make."*

Obama went on to explain that the act of making a single decision erodes your ability to make later decisions. And I feel this way too. I need to conserve my "decision making reserves" for the big things that only I can make.

I quickly learned the power of making one high-quality decision that removes the need to make multiple smaller decisions over the course of each day/week/month/year. This gives me so much more mental capacity to rest, relax or direct my thoughts on things that need focused attention.

Marketing is an area where we are faced with an impossible number of choices. This leads to an abundance of *"coulds"*, "*shoulds*" and "*oughts*" that don't serve us, or our purpose. What does serve us to sift through their clutter of possibilities, so we come to that one high-quality decision that is going to have the highest leverage for us. Because we could all do countless things, but that just leads to overwhelm, inaction, procrastination and ultimately guilt and shame. And we are not here for any of that.

This is why, if you are a personal brand, if you can't feed and sustain your most basic marketing system in an hour of your time each week, it's too much.

The power of a simple, powerful, strategic, aligned decision can be game-changing for your business, practice or consultancy. Making a few large decisions that save some of the 35,000 daily decisions and helps you create the spaciousness to be a thriving, healthy and vibrant individual.

When you are marketing yourself as a brand, it's important that you not only have a consistent, sustainable, easy-to-implement system in place, but you also protect "you" as the brand, and the mental energy you need to live and be your best.

Just Add Walnuts

For over a year I've been working with a world-class medically trained health coach and wholeness expert. The experience has been transformational and improved my health, energy and stress levels enormously. Before working with her I was reading books, blogs, watching videos, trying to piece together all the bits and pieces relevant to me: age, lifestyle, nutrition, movement, hormones, supplements, and a gazillion other things.

However, I lacked the insight of someone who had a holistic picture of my situation and who knew the ins and outs of all the different aspects of health way better than I did. When it came to my health, I was putting in the effort, but inwardly feeling unsure if my effort was being directed to the right place.

My health coach, Susan, is a multi-degree expert in genetics, neuroscience, biochemistry, as well as a naturopath who has run a wellness clinic for many years. So, what she could see in my situation was way more than I could, based on her experience and expertise. She has a wealth of knowledge, yet she doesn't overwhelm me with information, and that's the beauty of how she works. She gives me only what I can take in and do at any given time, and if that's too much, it gets pared back even more.

During a session with her last winter, I told her that I had deviated from the breakfast plan we'd discussed. Somehow on the cold winter mornings, I found myself going to oats, and loading it with butter and brown sugar. Sheepishly, I confessed this to Susan during my session.

Her response was extraordinary: *"That's great, at least you're eating, but there's one thing that I want you to do. When you make your oats, I want you to **grab a handful of walnuts** and add them to the dish because what's most important **for you right now** is protein in the mornings, and so if you do this – you have my full blessing to enjoy those oats – with butter, brown sugar, and WALNUTS!"*

Gosh I love this woman! This left me feeling great because there was no judgement, just encouragement, knowledge, and therefore power, as I now knew the ONE thing that really is going to make the most difference... for me, at that time. I couldn't do all the fancy-pants gourmet health concoctions, and on those cold winter mornings, cold smoothies were way less appealing than a bowl of warming oats. **But adding a handful of walnuts? Sure, I can do that.**

This brought home to me exactly why my approach works and the true power of simple when it comes to your marketing. With marketing, and getting your message out to more people, there are a million things you COULD be focusing on, all of which might work and make a difference.

The challenge for most people is working out which is the ONE THING that's going to make the most impact right now.

Susan knows what my body needs based on my lifestyle and bloodwork and genetics. She can see things that I can't see rather than me trying to figure it out on my own.

I was telling the clients in my *Marketing Me*® program about my walnuts experience recently. Recounting a conversation with a new client who had previously been trying to do "all the things" and who was feeling overwhelmed and frustrated, I shared my oats story –I then identified what I could see was the "one thing" she needed to do- and explained that her doing this "one thing" was akin to my "just add walnuts" example. In her case, it was to record a quick video in the park after she came out of a session with a particular client that lit her up and sparked ideas. The process from there had ease written all over it, and could take her insights and express them into the world – and she was clear on the "one thing" she needed to do each week. She felt that weight drop off her shoulders. It was so liberating, and it's become a beautiful way of highlighting this point.

For me at the moment, it's writing a weekly email to my community. That is the easiest place for me to create – and so if I do nothing else, I do that– and from there there's a process that will leverage that for blogs, and social posts which enables me to show up consistently, in multiple places, in less than an hour a week.

My mission for all of my clients is that everyone knows **the one thing they should focus on** now, **why it's important,** and **how it's going to move the needle.** It's also ever so considerate for your audience.

Reflection Question:

What's one marketing decision you could make (that would be easy to follow through on and take you max 1-hour/week) that if you did it every week your business would be in a different place in 90 days' time?

PART IV

THE HUMAN
SIDE OF BEING
A BRAND

In *Section I,* we looked at why we need to build our personal brand and what makes up a powerful and connected brand. In *Section II,* we looked out how to explore and express our unique identity and build confidence and influence. Then, in *Section III,* we looked the four practical areas to take action in, and where to start and what to do for each. Now, in *Section IV,* we take a look at "being the brand" – and this is important because your brand is only as vibrant as you are.

The human side of being a brand is all about protecting and nurturing your most valuable asset – you! It's less about business growth, marketing and all that jazz, because keeping you in a good place is mission-critical to being able to show up and market yourself and your business.

All the self-awareness in the world, your brilliance, depth of expertise, and even robust marketing systems won't serve you if you aren't able to remain emotionally buoyant. You must balance your work and brand building with the rest of your life.

I know this first-hand, having supported myself and many, many others through my businesses for 23 years, since I founded my first company. As a parent to five children, I'm well familiar with the full assortment of emotional, financial, time, and physical demands that comes with that – especially in the tougher seasons of life. I'm fully human and, like you, get tired, have overwhelming moments, frustration, and everything else that is a completely normal part of the human experience.

Over the years I've learned a few things about how to navigate this tricky journey of integrating business, family, and life – and **living a "life by design" rather than a life by default**. This means taking intentional steps to create a life that aligns with our values and priorities.

We all face challenges, experience down-days, and have moments of frustration. It's a completely normal part of the human existence and doesn't need to negatively impact on our personal brand. Yet the pursuit of intentional living and creating a life by design yields such great dividends. It's worth the relatively little effort we put into achieving the balance that leads to a fulfilling and rewarding life, infused with adventure, fun and joy.

CHAPTER 16

Nurturing Your Brand From Within

The challenge of building a personal brand with staying power is very real. Where we are all just so overloaded, it feels like stuff is coming at us non-stop, and the rate of change is relentless; we were not built for this. Sometimes, we honestly have to just do the minimum, put one foot in front of the other and that's about all we can do.

Know this: if you're feeling tired, and business or even life in general just seems like a lot, you are NOT alone. Be gentle to yourself. Just living day to day is a lot of effort, even without the added intensity of running a business, let alone the pressure to grow it.

I've always been a big believer in seasons of life and business. In seasons like we are in now, it's important to be present to what's going on. When external circumstances affect how we show up, what we do, how much time we're inside/outside, what we eat, our energy levels, as well as how we need to look after ourselves, we need to be aware of the toll these things take on us as humans.

So, in these times, how do you look after you when you're growing a business as well as doing everything else on your plate?

The Power of Intention

I've experienced and am living proof of the power of intention.

In 2016, I embarked on my personal brand journey with no idea of what was to follow. All I knew is that I was going to find, or, if necessary, create a path that worked for me. To do this required intention, it required me to set aside time to ask questions and think.

One of the most powerful examples of this was in January 2017, when I pondered the question: ***If I can be anything, what do I desire to be?*** A big question, for someone who was fairly set in their ways professionally. On that occasion, I took a couple of weeks to think this through, and at the end of that time there were two big things that emerged loud and clear. I want to be a CREATOR and CONNECTOR.

In all transparency, I didn't have much if any idea what that was going to look like. What I would be creating? Who I would be connecting with? What would it even mean? I didn't have the answers, but what that exercise did for me was help me start to plot the journey – it gave something for my intention to latch onto.

From there, the rest were just details, pulling themselves into place. I wish I could say I made it happen – in some respects I kind of did - but mostly things unfolded and I just went with whatever felt aligned during that time, trusting my intention was pulling me forward.

I didn't get a road map, far from it. More like a fuzzy telescopic view of a destination, but it was so blurry and vague I wasn't even able to recognise it, much less work out where it was or how to get there. BUT what it did do was instil the courage that was needed to take steps, and I feel that this deep intention was what pulled me forward. Sometimes consciously, mostly unconsciously.

I believe this power of intention isn't something limited to just building a personal brand, even though we all have one. It's way beyond that, linked to doing what we love in life. If something is boring and a chore, I've got the fortitude to apply myself to do a task as it's necessary, but I sure as anything don't want to be locked into doing it for the rest of my working life.

I choose to see all that we do in our professional lives as a *Choose Your Own Adventure* book. I loved these books as a child, and if I think about why – it's the sense of adventure, certainly, but beyond that, it's the notion of possibility, and if we really get down to it, the feeling of control.

My favourite in the series was *The Abominable Snowman*, and I remember going over the pages, testing out every ending, making sure I explored every possibility, to the point that pages were tired and worn out. But equally, if I wanted a short read it was a low-commitment way to experience a great story!

Reading those books, it felt amazing to be able to choose whatever outcome I felt and, moreover, if I didn't like how it panned out, go back to the beginning and start again!

This is a bit like what intention setting is like, except you don't just choose from a pre-set script, it's you that writes the words on the page too. You get to pick and choose the paths, the stories, the endings, and the number of times you go through the adventure itself. You always have the option to wind up that story start a completely new one.

When I thought about being a Creator – the word didn't have the meaning it does today – ubiquitous with digital savvy personal brand influencers. At the time I didn't know what I wanted to create. I didn't even see myself as a creative person up until that time. Of course, now I know that this was based on my own limiting belief about me not being creative simply because I'm not good at drawing, which held me back for way too long. Another version of the fear of standing out, which was overcome by embracing and expressing your unique identity, and leaning into my own unique expression of creativity and what I wanted it to mean for me.

So, what I have I created since then?

Brands, opportunities, experiences, content, videos, writings (hello!), graphics, programs, workshops, courses, routines, systems, a life by design... just to name a few.

As I reflect, I see that so much of what I do now is exactly the expression of that intention set back in 2016. Your dream and your most desired professional path is probably different to mine. And so, the takeaway here is that you don't always need to know where you're going to end up or even the path to get there, when you dream about what it is you want to do. You just need to harness the desire strongly enough and allow it to pull you into your future. Just start taking actions in alignment with that. Start creating, start walking, start exploring. And even if you're nervous you might just find you really enjoy it and find your stride!

The same can be said for becoming a Connector.

Unlike becoming a creator, I did have some context around what being a connector would mean for me. I have always had the ability to connect with people and having meaningful connections is something that comes naturally to me. Networking, connecting people with opportunities, connecting people to each other, and connecting people with their purpose. As a mentor in so many contexts in the course of my life, connecting has flown very naturally out of me and brought much joy. So, of course, this featured in everything I did over the years, professionally as well.

However, when it came up in the course of what I really wanted to do professionally, it was different because it wasn't part of what I did... yet. But there was a clear desire to make it what I did. So I just took micro-actions where I was, with actions that aligned with being a "connector" – even when I couldn't see how it would all come together.

I would say that this is absolutely what I do now. I connect people with their purpose. With opportunities. With each other. With possibility. With their audiences and clients. With their message. With the future they are stepping into.

I create. I connect.

It's purely and simply what I do. There's not a lot outside of these that I do, practically speaking, at its core this is what it all comes back to.

Why is this an important thing to talk about in the context of personal branding and marketing yourself? Having intention is a big part of not being aimless as you move forward and build that brand, and using personal branding to unlock the purpose, passion and potential in your life.

Eventually you'll say and do things that align with the future you desire to create, without realising it. If you can harness the power of intention and bring that into your world as well, it will be like adding rocket fuel to your thoughts and harnessing the energy like magnets that will pull you into that future faster than you realise.

Growth is Inevitable

This book isn't intended as a personal development book, but the very nature of putting yourself out there as a brand and attracting the right people to the world will require a healthy self-image and translate into a lot of personal growth. You can have all the expertise, credentials, and brilliance – even the heart and intention to help people and change lives.

But there's one more ingredient that is important to mention: self-worth.

That's right, valuing yourself.

On the one hand, it seems so obvious – of course you know you have value, otherwise you wouldn't even be on this journey of marketing yourself. On the surface, I'm sure you're an excellent business leader, service provider, CEO, entrepreneur, or employee, otherwise you probably wouldn't be reading this book in a quest to grow your personal brand. Yet, what you believe about yourself extends way deeper than your professional expertise, industry accolades, and desire to help.

If you're feeling like there's a disconnect somewhere, that's totally normal. For so long, I couldn't figure out what the disconnect was between having all the right ingredients, track record, and even pure motivations and experiencing the commercial success I desired through my brand.

We all hold deep-seated beliefs around whether we feel worthy to receive the success that the personal brand we desire to build is leading us into. This isn't only directly related to personal branding, it's equally true for living our best life in relationships, health, and all other aspects.

You are embarking on a personal quest to explore what underlying factors might be in play. What it uncovers is likely to surprise you, and probably challenge you – even the very act of being intentional about "wanting to know" will call in answers and revelation over time. But as you embrace these you will grow through them, and that growth will serve you in every aspect of your life.

This is not a self-help book. It's a book about how to build a powerful professional brand. But it would be remiss of me not to mention that a healthy self-worth and a willingness to stretch and grow are necessary ingredients in a successful personal brand.

Self-Care is Strategic

The most underrated factor for business performance as a personal brand is self-care.

It's not always convenient, and it takes strength to take time out when there are a gazillion things to do.

We may have in place streamlined service delivery, smart marketing systems, and the ability to prioritise what's really important in our business or career. But sometimes life happens, and we go through a season of levelling up (aka the messy stuff!).

The only way to get through it is to embrace it, be curious about what it's teaching us and what the lesson/gift in the situation is. Personally, I've found that often means taking time out from my already compacted business time to process the emotional and very human side of life.

I remember one time, I was so pumped to get into an exciting and significant business project. Lined up and prepped, I was ready to go. "To do" list on hand, fresh notebooks at the ready, and whole lot of enthusiasm.

Late the night before, I had a conversation that was very raw and deep, where someone I cared about challenged my thinking. It was around a few areas of my professional life and some beliefs I held, and that meant I had been operating way less impactfully than I had the potential to. Hearing that was confronting and made me sad, although I knew it came from a place of love, was healthy, and growth was going to come through it. I knew it would be instrumental in taking me to another level of clarity in my business.

It was tough to hear at the time. I wasn't at my best and was overcome with emotion. (I also had had a very rough few days in the parenting department.) And what that meant, was on my big "focus day" I had little ability to actually focus.

Having been in business for myself for 20+ years, there's one lesson I learned in more recent years that I wish I learned much earlier. **Let go.** Don't push through (unless you're obligated by a commitment you've made to a client or something where it wouldn't be the honourable thing not to show up). These days, when I find myself in that "processing" space, I get much better at asking myself what I need, and exploring what self-care would look like in that moment.

On that particular day, it looked like a picnic at the beach. I didn't view it as "time off". I saw it as deep recalibration, which enabled everything else in my business and life to function better. It made the remaining work hours in my week exponentially more fruitful. And made me a happier person, which is good for my family too.

I now make it a priority to have business "buffer time" at the ready so I am able to do this "recalibration" whenever I need to. Sometimes it's not required for a few weeks or months, other times I find myself doing it on a regular basis. I have dedicated days and times built into my week to be able to do this and it's been a lifeline in helping me become emotionally healthy, and giving myself space when I need it most.

Sometimes, the most important thing you can do for your business is *nothing*.

CHAPTER 17
Navigating the External Factors

Finding Your Sweet Spot

The year was 2001. I had established my marketing agency, *Braveda,* the year before and was at a conference working with start-ups. I was sitting in on a session presented by a management consultant, when I first heard the term "sweet spot". The consultant explained to the room that a sweet spot originated from a tennis term when you find that perfect spot on the racket that is the easiest to hit and gives you the most control and power over the ball as you strike it.

While I understood the term on the surface, it wasn't until a decade and a half later that it started to take on way more meaning in my own life. I finally came to realise that the ideal business or profession is one that strikes the right balance of:

- **what you're good at**
- **what you enjoy**
- **what pays well**
- **what's in demand**

The Japanese word for this is *Ikigai*, meaning your "reason for being" and it encompasses your purpose and your "bliss". Of course, laced through that is what is going to create impact and legacy. This dovetails in with what you enjoy, because it's deeply connected to your bigger purpose and that creates so much meaning and satisfaction. And when you are operating in this space, it's so much easier to create your brand because being in your sweet spot makes everything feel lighter.

Knowing vs Applying

While I did hear the term "sweet spot" much earlier and I really love the *Ikigai* philosophy, there's a difference between mental assent (i.e. assent at an intellectual level), and deeply embracing the concept to the point where it informs your actions, and you live from that place.

I spent much of my professional life accepting that if I could achieve two of those *Ikigai* points that was good enough and I should be happy with that. As a result, I feel like I short-changed myself and, in some instances, my family too.

I wasn't always achieving the same two or three, I traversed all of them in-and-out in different seasons. Sometimes doing what I didn't really love with all my heart, simply because it paid nicely. Other times, throwing caution to the wind and pursuing what I loved at all costs. Then there were times I identified a very clear market need and went about solving it. I was constantly yo-yoing between all of them repeatedly.

Something changed around the same time I got very intentional about building a personal brand that creates and connects. I set out a clear intention that I wanted to pursue a professional life which would deliver all four, no longer settling for two, or even three. I can't say it happened overnight but, eventually, it did. As I started to be intentional, each step and equally each misstep (there were plenty of those), took me closer to that reality.

The journey will be different for everyone who is building a personal brand, but here are a few of the common things I've observed in everyone I know that lives this reality, including myself.

Contrary to what we are often led to believe, stepping into our professional bliss is **NOT about:**

- ✘ More Hustle and Grind
- ✘ Trying to find that one, silver-bullet tactic
- ✘ Finding a business guru who promises the world and lets you in on their "secret"

Instead, it's way more about:

- ✓ Leaning into the BELIEF that it's possible – for you!
- ✓ Setting a clear INTENTION
- ✓ MINDSET upgrades

- ✓ SKILLSET upgrades
- ✓ Backing yourself when you take big RISKS
- ✓ Seeing "failures" as doorways that will release new OPPORTUNITIES
- ✓ ENVIRONMENTS that will reinforce and reflect your new normal
- ✓ Perseverance to keep your FOCUS where it needs to be
- ✓ Patience to STAY THE COURSE

Don't be fooled into thinking the whole process can be done and dusted in a few short weeks or months, regardless of what anyone says. The brand and the business focus go hand in hand. It's likely a journey of years but, like the saying goes, we overestimate what we can do in a week but underestimate what can be done in a year!

And here's the bottom line – if you never start you'll never get there.

The Importance of Timing

Anyone in Australia or New Zealand who watched TV in the 90's will have that iconic Pantene shampoo ad etched into their memory. "It won't happen overnight….but it will happen" And the same is true when it comes to building your personal brand. You don't become a thought leader and industry icon overnight. But when you're consistent, with the right elements, it WILL happen.

So often, we want things on our terms instead of being prepared to be patient and wait for the right time for things to happen. For those who are actively pursuing their dreams with everything in them and feel frustrated because it's just not working, no matter what you do, remember what we see is not the full picture of what's going on, just like looking at an ocean doesn't reveal the teeming life beneath the surface.

Sowing and reaping. Seedtime and harvest.

Seasons are one of the eternal, timeless laws of nature that impacts our entire planet. It is what our nutrition and sustenance is based on. It's also a rhythm that spans way beyond that, into every area of our lives.

There is a season for everything under the sun. Yet if you want to "reap" something, you just can't expect to do it if you don't plant the seeds. Planting the seeds takes faith, trust, hope, hard work and even after you've done all of that – a heck of a lot of patience. Even when your seeds start growing, you can't see it. You just have to know it's happening and trust that what you planted (and continue to water, tend and nurture) will come to fruition.

There's no way to bypass natural laws, even business "overnight successes" are the culmination of years, even decades of work in the background – it's just the majority of people are oblivious as to what goes into it. Then there's the "flash in the pan" superstar: the one who stumbles onto something being in the right place at the right time, and they're presented with an opportunity. However, it's short lasted and they fade away as quickly as they surfaced. Once the tough times come, they don't have the deep roots that have been strengthened over the years – the character that has been forged, the wisdom to build something lasting – that will underpin their decisions and which are ultimately responsible for overall quality of life.

If you're planting a field, there's no escaping the fact that you need to buy seed, prepare the soil, plant carefully, water and nurture, protect your sprouting crop from birds and pests and feed your crops. We need to follow the same metaphorical process as we grow our businesses. The journey might take longer than expected, or be less linear, or just plain hard. But know that if you keep going and pursue your passion and your purpose, putting one foot in front of the other you'll get there. Eventually.

In the meantime, work to reframe any feelings of stuck, frustrated, and disappointed with the knowledge that this is your training ground and it's the patience, persistence, and character that you forge. That's going to be the fuel that keeps you going when you finally take off. So, keep going!

The thing is, the next season is around the corner.

Success grows as you tend to your brand through all seasons.

Just like the farmer who continues to plant their seeds, knowing there are "natural cycles", **and they have faith in nature's ability to grow the seed** – so too it is with our business, our brand, and what we choose to do in our career and professionally.

This is my encouragement in the midst of whatever you've got going on.

- **Keep planting those seeds.**
  (share your awesome content with the world)
- **Keep watering your soil.**
  (staying in touch with and encouraging your customers and community)
- **Keep nurturing those seedlings.**
  (stay the course with your basic marketing – don't just do things ad hoc or up and down knee-jerk things – find something you can do on rinse-and-repeat with ease – and do it consistently)
- **Keep tending those growing plants.**
  (feeding and nourishing, and strengthening that brand of yours, that's emerging and becoming more visible in the world)

Some time ago I lived in New Zealand, near the water, where the soil was extremely fertile. I could plant any decent seed and within weeks vibrant lush plants would spring up. As someone who does not have a green thumb and had tried countless times to set up a vegetable garden in both Sydney and Melbourne, and never had more than mediocre success, this was a dream come true.

I was fully aware that the output wasn't because of my phenomenal gardening ability – but because of the quality and richness of the soil, and the climate.

Right now, the marketplace "soil" is very fertile!

And if you're following the principles I've outlined in this book, you'll have good quality seeds to plant, and tools to tend and nurture your plants.

So you can trust that as you keep planting the right seeds, and have faith in the natural process, you *will* reap the harvest.

Embracing a Cultivator's mindset

Being curious, trying new things and experimenting is essential if you want to build a personal brand, but the reality is sometimes these things work and sometimes they don't. And that's ok. To build a brand, you need to be willing to put yourself outside your familiar zone, stretch beyond where you have previously been comfortable, and show up in a way that causes you to expand and grow. Fully embracing your humanity and imperfections.

*"Don't let success go to your head,
and don't let failure get to your heart."*
— Beyonce

But in case you're still feeling any resistance, here's a word of reassurance.

People aren't as bothered about what you create and share as you think they are. Don't have a knee-jerk reaction and stop doing something after 1 or 2, or even 5 or 10 attempts. You need to give something a good 60-90 days to be able to see if it moves in a positive trajectory. You also want to collect enough data to identify trends and patterns. But if you don't give it a go, or if you stop too soon, you'll never know!

The Ultimate Destination is a Moving Target

Where you end up is inevitably going to be very different from where you imagine you will end up when you start.

The struggles you go through are part of the process, and for most people, you simply have to figure it out as you go. I love the quote, "begin with the end in mind" from Steven Covey's book *The 7 Habits of Highly Effective People*.[11]

On the one hand, we do want to have a clear idea of the direction we want to go in and the outcome we are pursuing, what it will ultimately look like is going to require flexibility and surrender on our part. There are so many factors that are beyond our control, that even if we had a plan and things went according to that plan, we still can't possibly even imagine what new opportunities the future will bring.

So, of course, when we are building our personal brand, we just don't know what the end is going to look like. And even if we did, what "end" would we be talking about anyway? 5 years' time? 10 years? 20 years? 50 years?

Not to mention that in that time our world will change in ways beyond what we can comprehend right now – and that's going to have a very clear impact on our opportunities, our focus, and what we decided to do.

So, I believe your definition of your "end" needs to change – albeit temporarily. Accept that the "end" is a moving target, and be flexible and fluid when designing your long-term strategy as a personal brand.

Over the years, I've pivoted several times before really finding my stride as a business brand. Even with my extensive marketing experience, setting out to build a personal brand and a business by design ultimately came from taking messy, imperfect action. I grew a lot through each experience by taking that action, in the best way I could at the time and releasing the need to get it right all the time (or even most of the time!).

I tried plenty of things that didn't work and, along the way, discovered lots of things that did. As Thomas Edison so rightly said, "I have not failed. I've just found 10,000 ways that won't work." That is me. Exactly. It still is, as I experiment on a daily basis to forge a path that isn't a direct copy of someone else.

I got comfortable with doing things that don't work because I had to, but don't mistake things that don't work with random things. The difference is that there was a clear and definite objective behind each of the actions I took, even at the beginning, when I didn't know what the end goal would look like. As I've gone along, I've been able to refine my strategic approaches many times to adapt to this crazy new fast-evolving, Wild West, 21st century business landscape.

And the invitation is beckoning for all of us to rise and chart our course, while being ready to adapt to the moving target ahead of us.

Baby step your way to your brand success

If building your brand is a journey, that itself, implies motion from A to B. We now know that "B" is a moving target, something you never arrive at, as the destination keeps shifting. The point to remember is though, is you're moving.

So how do you move? Through Steps.

Steps take you from one place to another. With steps you can change direction, increase your pace, slow down, "pivot" as required (to use a massively overused word). You can also Stop – simply by refusing to take steps.

So what are your steps? **Your steps into your future are**

your decisions and your thoughts. One by one they come, and not just the big ones. The big steps in life are things like what job do I do, what business do I start, what do I want to be known for? But the small steps are the ones that take you into the place from which you can make the big steps from a powerful position.

These small steps are happening all day, every day. Do I spend all my free moments in front of a screen or do I create space to pursue my dreams? Do I allow seeds of worry to take root in the soil of my mind and grow, or do I arrest those thoughts and make a decision to take a step back, assess rationally, and dream about what could be instead of what is?

Your confidence, self-worth and value come from who you see yourself to be.

"Whether you believe you can, or you can't – you're right" (Henry Ford)

"Everything is possible to the one who believes" – King James Bible (Mark 9:23)

Know that you can do it! Because you absolutely *can.* Don't start trying to move the mountain, start by mastering the mindset. Then break it down further, work on those thoughts you think on a regular basis, the daily thoughts that determine how you see yourself. The rest will follow.

Your Brand Matters

Of all the phrases you never, ever want to hear in an operating theatre, *"I want you to know we are going to try and do everything we can"* would be at the top of my list.

Earlier on in the day on which I heard that dreaded phrase, I had been admitted to a small maternity hospital to deliver my first baby. He was breech, exceptionally large, and there were some complications, so I followed the medical advice and agreed to a caesarean section.

Excited for the big day, I remember "dropping in" to the supermarket on the way to the hospital to buy some flowers for my doctor.

"So, what are you up to today?" said the cashier as I paid for the flowers and chocolates.

"Oh, I'm on my way to go and have a baby now!" I said enthusiastically. Not a response she hears too often so we had a bit of a chuckle, and I continued on to the hospital.

I checked into my room, the heavy fabric curtains, plush pattered quilt cover, nursing chair and muted pastel décor providing a sense of warmth and comfort, as I unpacked my bag and laid out the newborn clothes ready for the impending arrival.

That was the memory I had – although in this moment there was no baby, no clothes, and no plush curtains.

A sense of disorientation enveloped me as I awoke in a haze, my surroundings a blur.

Scanning the room, there was nothing that reminded me of that hospital room I'd been in earlier. Flashing lights and high-tech machinery all around. The muted pastels had been replaced by bright white walls and hospital sheets. The nurses uniforms were different. My own gown was different. And this hospital room was a lot bigger. The only thing I could be sure of amid the confusion was that this wasn't the hospital I was supposed to be in.

The words I attempted to utter—"Where's my baby?"—were stifled, reduced to incoherent mumbles that struggled to break free from my lips. My mind attempted to piece together the fragments of memory that slowly came into focus. I found myself amidst a sea of hospital beds, the hustle of doctors and nurses like a whirlwind around me. It didn't make sense.

The last memory I had was having my firstborn baby boy. So how did I get here? And how much time has passed? And the biggest question of all.....what the heck happened?

I suddenly became aware of the volume of apparatus attached to my own body, which spoke of a story I couldn't yet comprehend. As I slowly regained consciousness, I gestured to the nurse to give me a pen and paper so I could communicate. The nurse handed me paper, and a pencil ....

"Where is my baby?" I swiftly wrote, in handwriting resembling a 4-year old's.

The response came with a reassuring swiftness: "Don't' worry, your baby is fine and being looked after, but you're in intensive care."

Slowly I began to ask questions, the answers to which started filling in the blanks and my mind was cast back to birth of my son.

After a straightforward c-section, and having my first newborn cuddles and feed, I was told the nurse was going to take the baby to the other room for a few minutes while they completed the procedure, and that I'd be reunited with my baby in about half an hour.

The routine post-birth procedures commenced. Except there was very little "routine" about what happened next.

My uterus did not contract as it was expected to after delivering a baby. I began to haemorrhage and could see the concern in the operating staff's eyes, which quickly escalated to panic.

They were trying one thing after the next and nothing seemed to work. I could see them giving urgent messages to hospital staff, asking them to call different people, specialists to see who could come in immediately and help. It was late on a Friday night by this time.

The last thing I remember was the doctor and anaesthetist saying *"we need to put you under anaesthetic now, and know we are going to try and do everything that we can...we'll do our best....".*

I later learned two more doctors came in so there were three obstetricians, with a combined 50 years' experience in obstetrics working together in the operating theatre. Because the uterus did not contract, I had lost so much blood that it had escalated to a critical level where they were now trying to find a way to save my life.

My obstetrician had made a call which was a very brave one – one I will be forever grateful for – which was not to remove my womb – which at the time was the conventional option in this situation. She knew it was my first baby, and that I wanted more children. She said she knew how devasted I would be waking up to find out my womb had been removed, and she was ready to do whatever she could to find another way.

That "way" involved bringing in a specialist who had heard of, what was then, a brand new medical alternative to a hysterectomy in women who had post-partum haemorrhaging. A procedure called a B-Lynch suture, developed by Sierra-Leone born surgeon Dr. Christopher B-Lynch.

It wasn't mainstream medical procedure yet, and I was later told that one of the obstetricians was searching the internet at the hospital reception desk prior to operating to read up on the procedure and explore whether it would be feasible to attempt in my situation. Seems it was, and I was told I was the first person in Australia to undergo this procedure, and the sixth person in the world. (It's worth noting – and celebrating! – that this procedure has since saved the lives of two million women in childbirth, according to the World Health Organisation).

The way I became aware of what had transpired, was when a curious young nurse in the intensive care ward showed me a medical diagram printed from the internet – after he had heard what happened and googled it himself. I sensed he felt like quite the hero, informing me with the help of the internet print out. What I could make out was that the hospital staff were abuzz with curiosity about this new procedure, and the woman whose life it had saved. It didn't all make sense to me at the time but over the following days it started to piece together.

I was told about the catastrophic blood loss. Medical records showed I had lost 3.5 litres (almost a gallon) of blood. I learned I was transported by ambulance from the suburban maternity hospital to a big city hospital with a large intensive care unit for a blood transfusion.

As it turns out, despite such heavy blood loss, upon arrival at intensive care, my vital organs had stabilised on their own, and my iron count was steadily rising on its own, so the decision was made not to do a transfusion – which itself was risky as to replace more than half of someone's blood can cause other complications.

In intensive care, I was hooked up to all the monitoring devices and had medical staff permanently stationed next to my bed, monitoring the vast array of machines, watching carefully for any signs of organ failure.

And then, sometime later, I woke up.

Shortly after I had enquired about my baby on the paper, I went back into a coma. I'm not sure how long passed but the next memory I had was of my obstetrician, standing over me, crying. *"I don't know if I ever really believed in God"* she said *"But I do now"*.

We shared a beautiful moment together, and it was not long after that I found out the full medical implications of what had happened.

As the days rolled on, clarity returned, and the miracle of my survival became more apparent. A cascade of emotions engulfed me—gratitude, relief, wonder. The birth of my child had intertwined with a battle for life, my story now intertwined with the legacy of medical innovation. And a renewed sense of awe just for being here.

I'm thankful this story had a beautiful end.

And several beginnings too

Four more beautiful children, to start with.

Miracle after miracle.

I went on to have four more children (all VBAC, for those that are familiar with that).

And today I have a lively household, and count myself extremely blessed each day.

But it doesn't stop in my household. Thanks to the life-saving, womb-saving invention of Dr B-Lynch, who refused to be limited by the conventional wisdom of the time, and who was intent on pursuing a better way despite the traditional training, more than 2 million women worldwide and counting have had a different ending to the one that otherwise would have been.

And the ripple effect of two million lives saved, countless more children born to those women, and the families, communities and countries that have been changed as a result.

What transpired over the following years was a relentless sense of stewardship over this life I've been given. And a desire to do things differently and forge a new path. Not just because of what happened during the birth, but because it kickstarted a series of events and circumstances that led to me connecting to a deeply-held desire which was always in me, to create impact globally.

Since that time, the impact my work has had is beyond what I can comprehend. Not because I'm famous, or speak in stadiums, or am a prolific author. The book you hold in your hands (or on your screen) is my first. But I care deeply about the work I do. And the people I serve. And the ripple effect on the people they serve.

"I want my kids, and their kids, and other people's kids, to grow up in a world full of inspiring voices of strength and substance, a world with a plethora of aspirational role models."

I wrote these words in the Introduction to this book. As the desire to amplify positive voices in the world is my motivation for building and being a brand.

I have found that, for me, amplifying positive voices in the world is easy, primarily because it's not something I 'do', it's simply who I am.

If you'd like to market yourself with as little effort as possible, my encouragement to you is to discover, embrace, and express who you are.

"IF YOUR BRAND DISAPPEARED TOMORROW, WHAT WOULD THE WORLD BE MISSING?"

If it were not for Dr B-Lynch and his refusal to accept conventional wisdom, millions of women and children would be missing from the world, and the futures and lives they have created.

If it were not for my doctor, who intently pursued another way from the conventional approach, I would not have the family I do today, which are a huge part of the reason behind why I do what I do.

It's often in the most challenging and unprecedented times where conventional wisdom fails that we're awakened to new possibilities and our latent passions.

We are in unprecedented and challenging times now, and conventional approaches aren't working. In marketing, in business, and in the economy.

Now is the moment to create your future.

By being curious.

Trying new things.

Not accepting the status quo.

And above all, by tapping into your identity, and your desires.

Through understanding and embracing who you are. And expressing that into the world.

Your uniqueness, your significance.

More than just being a thought leader.

It's time to be a life leader.

It's time to be uniquely, fully, you.

References

1   Moonlanding Agency

2   Simpson, J. (2017, August 25). Finding brand success
     in the digital world. *Forbes*. https://www.forbes.
     com/sites/forbesagencycouncil/2017/08/25/
     finding-brand-success-in-the-digital-world

     Bloomtools. (2022, January 27). 23 Recent PPC stats important
     for Australian businesses in 2022. *Website design, Email Marketing
     & CRM solutions*. https://www.bloomtools.com/blog/23-re-
     cent-ppc-stats-important-for-australian-businesses-in-2022

3   Greek Philosopher Heraclitus.

4   Schaefer, M. (2023, February 4). *You can't be an expert. And
     you don't have to be.* Schaefer Marketing Solutions: We Help
     Businesses Grow. https://businessesgrow.com/2023/01/23/
     expert/

5   Carl W. Buechner, and often attributed to Maya Angelou.

6   *2020 KPMG Women's Leadership Summit Report announcement.*
     (2020, October 12). KPMG. https://womensleadership.kpmg.us/
     summit/kpmg-womens-leadership-report-2020.html

7   Clance, P. R., & Imes, S. A. (1978). The imposter phenomenon in
     high achieving women: Dynamics and therapeutic intervention.
     Psychotherapy: Theory, Research & Practice, 15(3), 241–247.
     https://doi.org/10.1037/h0086006

8   Jamison, L. (2023, February 6). Why everyone feels like they're
     faking it. *The New Yorker*. https://www.newyorker.com/
     magazine/2023/02/13/the-dubious-rise-of-impostor-syndrome

9   Williamson, M. (2009). *A return to love: Reflections on the
     Principles of A Course in Miracles*. Harper Collins.

10   Clear, J. (2018c). *Atomic habits: the life-changing million-copy #1
     bestseller*. Random House.

11   Covey, S. R. (2004). *The 7 Habits of Highly Effective People:
     Powerful Lessons in Personal Change*. Simon and Schuster.

Additional Resources

Thank you for reading this book!

I trust it has given you the insights, inspiration and roadmap to building your own personal brand in a way that suits your unique personality & strengths, business or career goals, and lifestyle.

By scanning the QR code below you will be able to access book bonuses and additional resources that will support your personal brand journey.

(Or visit www.ninachristian.com/marketing-me-book)

Acknowledgements

Today, I reflect in awe of the journey that brought me here, the lives that intersected with mine, and the impact that has reverberated far beyond the realm of my own experience. The chapters of my life are not just my own, but a tapestry woven with the threads of others – infused with resilience, innovation, and the unstoppable force of life itself.

Firstly, and on a very practical note, I want to express my gratitude and appreciation to my children, my dear parents, and my dear aunt for your unwavering practical support as I wrote this book.

Thank you for your understanding and patience over the last year as I wrote, edited and published this book while doing all the "business as usual", and "mum as usual" stuff as best as I could.

My parents – no words to explain how much I love and appreciate you both, and all you've done for me and my children over many years. You have been there for me through thick and thin and have never wavered in your kindness and willingness to support me and the children. We are where we are today in a large part because of you.

Aunt Nadia – for stepping in to hold the fort when necessary and being such an important part of "the village".

To my clients – who I love so much, and who bring so much joy, inspiration and energy into my world.

My marketing peers, business colleagues and all the thought leaders I'm connected with, as well as all the wonderful people that make up my professional network – thank you for ongoing encouragement, support and inspiration.

Ben, Mish and the Hambone Publishing team – for your exceptional work in taking care of the logistical elements of getting this work into the world, and making the whole publishing journey easy and smooth. You have been extraordinary. Thank you.

I also extend my deepest gratitude to those who have been an important part of my book journey.

Alex, Matt, Lisa, Rowena, Col, Jane, Susan, Raneeta, Karina, Francine, Renee, Beth, Jen, Shane, Cat, Winitha, Monique & Selena.

Each of the people mentioned above has contributed in a significant way in helping to get these words from inside my head and heart, into the book you are holding in your hands (or reading on your screen).

Alongside that, several have played a key part over the last decade in helping me to personally explore the two big questions posed by this book:

WHO AM I – to myself?
WHO AM I – in the world?

I am a different person because of the quest I undertook in pursuit of these questions.

Maybe you can relate.

To a desire that has always been there.

Yet, somehow it doesn't feel outworked to its fullest.

And then, an event or series of circumstances comes along, which plays its (often painful) role in bridging desire and reality. It's always a process, and for me personally, it led me to connect with my identity in a way I never had before. And because of the work I do in marketing, I quickly realised the impact it has on a brand, especially when it's a personal one. And I can absolutely correlate the level of my impact to the level I had connected with and embraced my identity.

And in so doing, uncovering the answers to these two questions we explored in Chapter Two. Pursuing the answers to these powerful questions was the catalyst for my deep dive into the world of personal branding and positioning. Seeing that everything is related, and that the journey of uncovering who you are and how you express that is what causes the impact.

The impact my work has had is beyond what I ever dreamed it would. Not because I'm famous, or speak in stadiums, or am a prolific author. The book you are reading now is my first. But I care deeply about the work I do. And the people I serve. To me this impact feels gentle and easeful, but solid. And there is nothing in the world I would rather be doing. And it's why I'm so grateful I went through the journey I shared with you in this book - because it's enabled me to lead others through it as well.

Extraordinary people who have been drawn into my world, who have been infused with confidence, courage and conviction because they began to see who they really are. Who were then empowered to take bigger, bolder actions. And were inspired by my own messy, imperfect example of following a path that is not the traditional one, and forging their own. In fact, that's what's needed most. Passionate, messy, impact-driven trailblazers.

Their stories inspire me.

And it makes me so glad I chose the path I did.

Which circles back to the ultimate reason I do what I do, and why I wrote this book.

"I want my kids, and their kids, and other people's kids, to grow up in a world full of inspiring voices of strength and substance, a world with a plethora of aspirational role models."

I wrote these words in the Introduction to this book because it's my motivation for building a personal brand and teaching others how to "be the brand".

I'm clear on that. It lights me up, and brings me joy.

And best of all, discovering the thrilling and comforting

revelation that the greatest impact comes not through "doing" but primarily, just through "being" – when it's aligned with our true self.

As we live out and pursue a different way to "BE" in business and in life.

So I close out with this acknowledgement and dedication to you, the reader.

Thank you for reading this book.

Thank you for taking the courageous steps this book has led you through, and applying them in your own professional journey.

Here's to you and the impact you are creating.

May the world, and moreover *your* world, be a better place for it.

Much love

Nina

About the Author

Nina Christian is a marketing futurist, global marketing mentor, speaker, and change leader, who is all about doing marketing in a more human and energising way.

She weaves together her expertise of 20+ years as a marketing agency owner, building multiple brands of her own (including a successful exit), and being a hands-on parent to five children.

She is a Certified Practicing Marketer (CPM), Life Member and Fellow of the Australian Marketing Institute, Former AMI State Chair (Vic) and for 20 years was director of Braveda which was awarded Best Marketing Agency at the Australian Marketing Excellence Awards in 2018.

Several years ago Nina saw the world of marketing shifting – this time as people became their own brands. With this, she created a new business as a thought leader, combining her expertise in brand building with personal positioning, resulting in a breakthrough praxis known as Marketing Me® which she has been delivering globally to business leaders, professionals and entrepreneurs.

She is passionate about living a life by design and empowering those around her to "be" the impact they desire to see in the world.

Connect with Nina

www.ninachristian.com
www.linkedin.com/in/ninachristian

To book Nina to speak at your conference or event or to enquire about any of her programs & resources please reach out to support@ninachristian.com.